"The missing ingredient in modern Christianity centers around what we are willing to sacrifice so Jesus becomes readily apparent on His people. The tipping point for a sacrificial life is DISCIPLESHIP and that might be equally absent in North American Christianity. I'm excited about Rudy's book on "Heaven Colored Sunglasses", due to its radical, revelatory and discipleship nature. This book contains fresh explosive gems on a variety of themes that all center upon the Lord Jesus Christ and Kingdom expansion. True Kingdom expansion must take place internally before it takes place externally. Rudy brings this truth home in his own clear and unique style. I believe that you will be challenged by this work and will be launched into fresh exploits by this gifted vessel!"

Sean Smith
Author of "Prophetic Evangelism" and "I Am Your Sign"
@RevSeanSmith
www.seansmithministries.com

STOP LOOKING FOR YOUR BREAKTHROUGH AND LIVE IT!

*Heaven-Colored Sunglasses*

Rudy Topete

WEST BOW
P R E S S
A DIVISION OF THOMAS NELSON

ISBN: 978-1-4497-5351-1 (sc)
ISBN: 978-1-4497-5352-8 (e)
ISBN: 978-1-4497-5353-5 (hc)

Library of Congress Control Number: 2012909170

WestBow Press books may be ordered through booksellers or by contacting:

WestBow Press
A Division of Thomas Nelson
1663 Liberty Drive
Bloomington, IN 47403
www.westbowpress.com
1-(866) 928-1240

Printed in the United States of America

WestBow Press rev. date: 06/04/12

*I would like to dedicate this book to my son, Gabriel. I pray that this would encourage you to listen to the voice of God and let Him guide you in making your dreams a reality.*

*I would like to also dedicate this book to my wife Nikki for her love, support and willingness to go anywhere the Lord leads me...no matter how crazy it seems.*

# Acknowledgments

To God be all the glory and praise!

I would like to thank my parents for being a demonstration of endurance, love and hard work.

To my first mentor Pastor Andre Brackens. You taught me how to have a love for prayer, the Word and coached me as I learned to communicate at the pulpit. I am forever grateful for your love and encouragement.

To Pastor Steve Myatt, for shaping my adult spiritual life and fortifying my character as a man of integrity, honor and dedication. Life is different because of you, period.

To my mentor, friend and coach Robert Guerrero, "Just do it!" you showed me how and continue to do so. Thank you for your friendship and encouragement.

To my family, you have all blessed my family and me with more than we deserve.

To the staff and friends of Vista Assembly for your ongoing prayer, support, love and laughter. You have showed me how to be a better pastor, father, husband and friend.

To Michael (Mikey) Gonzales, thanks for all your hard work, laughs and amazing creativity.

To Holly my very first customer…you are reading this book from heaven, can't wait to get your feedback when I get there.

# Contents

# Introduction

A FEW YEARS AGO, WHILE serving as a youth pastor, I opened our midweek youth service the way thousands of youth groups begin—with an icebreaker. In this game I had several pictures on a PowerPoint presentation that would be revealed piece by piece until the entire image was uncovered. The object of the game was to guess what the picture was before the entire image was revealed. If a student could successfully identify the pictures before the image was revealed, they would win a free youth ministry T-shirt.

I asked for a volunteer, and a little fifth-grade girl raised her hand with an excitement like she was playing for a thousand dollars. I called her up, and she quickly made her way to the stage. She had no problem identifying the pictures and made it all the way to the very last round. In the final stage, I had a picture of Mickey Mouse with only a small portion of his ears showing. It took everything in me to keep the audience silent as to not give away the answer. She took some guesses but could not figure out what the image was. Because she was simply *adorable*, I gave her a hint. I said, "It's the happiest place on earth." Without hesitation and with brightness in her eyes, she yelled out, "Heaven?!" She won the T-shirt.

All our lives we have been taught that heaven is the place where we rest eternally in the very presence of God. It is a peaceful and joyous place as there is no sickness, sorrow, sin, or separation in heaven. Every tear will be wiped away, and we will no longer suffer from the constant wiles of the devil. When family members or friends pass away, we often comment on how they "are no longer suffering" and "are dancing with the angels." This is all real and comforting truth; however, it is my firm conviction that we don't have to wait until we get to heaven to experience the *realities* of heaven. In the model of prayer that Jesus gave to us in Matthew 6:10, He says, "Your kingdom come. Your will be done on **earth** as *it is* in **heaven**."

When Christians refer to what Jesus has done for them, it is always spoken in past tense. We say things like "Jesus died for all my sins" or "I *was* a sinner but *now* I'm saved." Yet our daily lives do not seem that much different from those who do not know Jesus. We accept sickness, depression, anger, sin, and many other things of the devil with no consideration as to what God has freely given to us and enabled us to do. The powerful truth is that we do not have to live a miserable, defeated, and hopeless life.

My soul comes alive when I am reminded in scripture of all that I have in Christ, who He is to me, and of my identity in Jesus. It's as if my spirit screams in agreement when I read passages like the following:

+ "I can do all things through Christ who strengthens me" (Philippians 4:13).

+ "I am more than a conqueror in Christ" (Romans 8:37).

+ "The devil has been completely defeated" (1 John 3:8).

+ "Nothing is too hard for God" (Genesis 18:14).

+ "I have every Spiritual blessing in Christ" (Ephesians 1:3).

+ "The Same power that raised Jesus from the grave lives is in me" (Romans 8:11).

I am encouraged and challenged by verses like these. They speak volumes to me and convince me that I am to live a continually victorious life that demonstrates God's love and power. I simply and confidently refuse to live in apathy, defeat, misery, or bondage. The death, burial, and resurrection of my Lord conquered everything that you and I will ever face in life, including the ultimate—death. For this reason, I can walk in joy that my God is bigger than anything I will ever encounter.

In this book, *Heaven-Colored Sunglasses,* I want to walk you through a very "101 style" teaching of how to walk with the perspective of heaven in all that you say and do—while on earth. I want to address some of the most critical misconceptions we believers have in the Christian faith. I want to dismantle the lies that the enemy has been feeding Christianity and reveal the clear and powerful Word of God. In this book you will

+ see that God's plan for believers has not changed since the Garden of Eden,

+ understand that God loves you and is not out to "get you,"

+ uncover *all* that Jesus purchased for you,

+ learn how to operate in your God-given authority,

- discover how pathetic and harmless the devil really is,

- learn how to walk in the Spirit, not in the flesh.

I could write an entirely separate book on all that I have seen God do in my life and in the lives of my family in this past year. When I began this project, I had walked away from ten years of full-time youth ministry. I was unemployed, living in a guest bedroom with family, and unsure of my identity in Christ. With a wife who was confident in her husband and together depending on God, we trusted for a miracle and moved forward in faith.

In one year's time we saw God bless us with a dream job in the ministry, financial blessing, family that came to the Lord, reconciliation between my wife and father, and received the keys to our very first home. The world will tell you it is impossible to get a job in this economy, yet a perfect position was handed to us. The enemy will try to lie in your ear that your relationships will never succeed, yet I have seen healing and salvation in my own family. The devil will try to hold you down with sickness, depression, and lack—but I have been convinced that nothing is impossible for my god.

I want to encourage you to take an open-minded and openhearted journey with me as we discover how to stop looking for our breakthrough and start living it! With *Heaven-Colored Sunglasses*, let us see and walk in the life we've always wanted.

# Chapter 1

## *No Plan B*

THERE ARE NOT TOO MANY places in the world where you can go surfing at the beach, enjoy a picnic at the park, go off-road driving in the desert, and ski down a mountain, all in the same day. There are many benefits to living in sunny San Diego, California, arguably the greatest year-round weather in the world. When you live in a place that is seventy-five degrees year round, it is nice to head up to the mountains once in a while and experience what another season is like.

I am blessed to have a family that owns a beautiful cabin in Big Bear Mountain, California. A while back, my family and I, as well as our close friends, took an extended weekend to enjoy a few days of relaxing, fishing, watching movies, and playing games. It is wonderfully refreshing to be away in a cozy cabin, feeling a million miles away from home and responsibilities.

Over the course of the few days on the mountain, the wives decided to put their minds together and attempt a thousand-piece jigsaw puzzle of the *Last Supper*. One . . . thousand . . . pieces. You could have started this puzzle during the *actual* last supper and still continue working on it today. What is amazing is that there are puzzles that are larger than just a thousand pieces. The puzzle was so big that our friend actually had a felt carpet to do the puzzle on so that if they didn't finish in one sitting, they could roll it up and save it for another time.

If you have ever been around a group of people attempting a puzzle, you know that there are several different methods and styles of putting a puzzle together. Some like to make a perimeter frame and work their way in, while others prefer to make patches of puzzle pieces to eventually join together. Some are very "type A" and enjoy counting and separating all the pieces by shade and color before they even begin joining the first two puzzle pieces. Regardless of what methodology you use to construct a puzzle, generally there is one rule that all must follow: looking at the picture on the box cover. It is almost a guarantee that anytime a puzzle is being worked on, somewhere nearby is the box top positioned for all to see. This serves as a point of reference so that everyone, at any point, can check their progress and make sure they are on track.

I like to imagine that the Christian life and body of Christ are much like a giant puzzle. There are many ideas today about how the church should operate and how the Christian life should be lived. There are many shades, colors, and styles, but all pieces must come together in unity to form the picture on the box. I am confident that all believers, regardless of denomination, background, or culture should have one focus in mind—living in the reality of heaven, today.

## God's Original Design

When God created the heavens, the earth, and mankind, He did so with a heart for relationship, compassion, and power. The kingdom of Heaven would be established for man on earth. There would be no sorrow, sickness, or sin. Man and woman would walk in the cool of the day with the Lord and commune with the God of Heaven. We were made in God's image and took on His characteristics and nature. Adam and Eve were given authority to rule over the earth and lived with no fear of the evil one or darkness. Take a look at the account in Genesis:

> *So God created man in His own image; in the image of God He created him; male and female He created them. Then God blessed them, and God said to them, "Be fruitful and multiply; fill the earth and **subdue** it; have **dominion** over."(Genesis 1:27–28; emphasis mine)*

You could say that Adam and Eve experienced heaven on earth and lived out God's intention and desire. Sadly, we all know that the story does not have a happy ending. Adam and Eve came into agreement with the serpent and through deception welcomed sin, death, and destruction into this world. From this point we see mankind in a downward spiral of sin and hopelessness. From there, God introduced the law through the prophet Moses, and we can read of Israel's roller-coaster ride with rebellion and obedience throughout the whole Old Testament.

Because of man's failed attempts at righteousness, Jesus came to our world to die for our sins once and for all. He set us free from the law and came to restore all that was lost. In essence, Jesus came to bring mankind back to the original plan.

> *And by Him everyone who believes is justified from all things from which you could not be justified by the law of Moses. (Acts 13:39)*

*And I will give you the keys of the kingdom of heaven, and whatever you bind on earth will be bound in heaven, and whatever you loose on earth will be loosed in heaven. (Matthew 16:19)*

## The Incredible Claims of the Bible

The Bible has some powerful and wonderful things to say about us despite our sin, actions, and past. It is amazing to read scripture like John 3:16 that speaks of the truth that "God so loved the *world* and that He gave His only Son." God loved us before we came to know Him and stopped at absolutely nothing to give us everything—even His one and only son. I love how Erwin McManus, pastor of Mosaic Church, says it, "One day you will stop running and turn around to find a God who has always been pursuing you." The most loving and powerful Person in the universe desires a relationship with you. We have such comfort and liberty knowing a massive and loving God hears our every cry and desires our fellowship.

Our loving Heavenly Father also blessed us with incredible help. Romans 8:11 says, "But if the Spirit of Him who raised Jesus from the dead dwells in you, He who raised Christ from the dead will also give life to your mortal bodies through His Spirit who dwells in you." Jesus Christ conquered the ultimate—death. The thing we all fear was conquered and destroyed (think about that). The same Spirit that raised Christ from the grave lives in you and me. In fact, the book of Romans goes on to say that we are "more than conquerors" (Romans 8:37). We are not just regular conquerors; we are *more than* conquerors because our bodies literally house the Holy Spirit, God Himself (1 Corinthians 3:16). We not only have a God that loves us, but we also have a death-conquering power that dwells in us.

Our circumstances must also bow to the name of Jesus and the identity He has given us. The Bible boasts in Genesis 18:14, "Is anything too hard for the LORD?" The book of Philippians gives us the promise that we can "do all things through Christ who gives us strength" (Philippians 4:13). I love how the Bible gives it to you straight and leaves no room for excuses. The revivalist Leonard Ravenhill says it just as bluntly as the scriptures, "One day some simple soul will pick up the Bible, read it, do it, and the rest of us will be embarrassed."

## The Normal Christian Life

When I read scriptures like the ones I just mentioned, I am simply convinced that the Christian life should be marked by power, favor, intimacy, and service. Nowhere should we see powerlessness, poverty, or lack in the Spirit-filled believer. God has gone above what we could even imagine and has given us all that we need:

> *And God is able to make all grace abound toward you, that you, always having all sufficiency in all things, may have an abundance for every good work. (2 Corinthians 9:8)*

My personal theory is that the church of Jesus Christ should walk and operate in the ways God originally established. We simply need to take things back to how it was in the beginning. In Mark chapter 10, some Pharisees come up to Jesus and question Him on divorce. They tested Jesus and asked if it is Lawful for a man to divorce his wife. Jesus responds by saying that though Moses permitted a certificate of divorce, it was due to the hardness of man's heart and that *from the beginning* God made them "male and female" and "therefore what God has joined together, let not man separate" (verse 9). Jesus was ultimately saying, "Live your life according to God's original establishments, not man's traditions." For the church to step into her rightful identity, we must simply look at God's original desire and the establishment of the first-century church.

The church in the book of Acts was marked with signs, wonders, miracles, service, and incredible devotion to God and His presence. As great as the advances have been for the modern church, we must never forsake the original intentions Jesus had for His bride, the church. We must dare to reach for the impossible and strive to release the power of God in all areas of our sphere of influence. The mega church pastor Joel Osteen says it beautifully at the beginning of every service, "This is my Bible, I am what it says I am and I can do what it says I can do."

## *Spreading His Kingdom*

In the Old Testament (old covenant of law), the greatest example of releasing the realities of heaven on earth, in my opinion, was King Solomon. During his reign as king, Israel experienced peace, prosperity, favor, and intimacy. There were no famines or wars, and Israel experienced a golden season of coming into alignment of God's blessing.

Solomon's father, King David, had it in his heart to build a temple for the Lord. Yet because of David's bloody reign, the assignment was given to his son, Solomon. In the account found in 1 Chronicles 22, I find some amazing truths that you and I can apply to help us advance the kingdom of God on earth.

*Now David said, "Solomon my son is young and **inexperienced**,
and the house to be built for the LORD must be **exceedingly
magnificent**, famous and glorious throughout all countries.
I will now make **preparation** for it." So David made
abundant preparations before his death. (emphasis mine)*

What a command! Here you have an inexperienced king who is told to build a house for *God* and it must be "exceedingly magnificent." Can you imagine the weight of responsibility on Solomon's shoulders? But what I love so much about God is that His requirement for spreading the kingdom of God is simply knowing Him. Our talents and intelligence do not qualify us, Jesus's blood qualifies us for kingdom work. God will use anyone who is willing.

I remember a while back I took a group of student leaders out into the community for some street evangelizing. As we gathered on the front steps of the church and circled up to hear from God on where He wanted us to go minister, a student went walking across our parking lot and stumbled upon our prayer meeting. This prayer event was only for student leaders, and this student had no clue as to what we were doing. He was literally walking through the parking lot on his way home. As he noticed us, he went over and asked what we were doing. I answered him with a bold statement in a poor attempt to scare him away from what we were doing (as it was a leadership event). I said, "Oh, we are asking *God* where He wants us to go, because we are going to go up to complete *strangers* and pray *out loud* for their needs." I thought that would be more than enough to scare any teenager away, but to my surprise he responded by saying, "Sweet! Can I come?" How do you say no to that kind of joy?

We all loaded up in our cars, and I had this student sit up front in my car so that I could literally teach him how to pray for others on the way to pray with strangers. As I was explaining and teaching, he cut me off and tried to summarize my comments by saying, "So you just ask God where and who He wants you to pray for and the first thing off the top of your head you go with?" I tried to backpedal and explain prayer a little more clearly, but before I could get another word in, he spotted a street sign that looked like the word Brooklyn. He then shouted, "All right, I need to find a little girl named Brooklyn and I will pray for her." I wanted to say, "Well, that's not exactly what I mean," but I thought I would leave it alone and see what happens.

We arrived at a strip mall in town and began splitting up in teams and walking around looking for people to pray with. As I was coming around a corner, I saw most of the leaders huddled around a Hispanic family. I went over to see the kids in action. I found my rookie prayer warrior in the middle of the group praying for a little girl about two years old. When he was finished praying, one of the leaders looked at me with a smile and said, "Her name is Brooklyn."

God doesn't need your résumé before you can spread His kingdom; He needs your heart and your willingness to be used by Him.

## Make Up Your Mind

One strong quality that many mighty men of God had in common was a mind that was made up. The prophet Daniel "resolved in his mind not to defile himself with the king's delicacies" (Daniel 1:8). Abraham was called to leave his home country and go into a foreign land. The book of Hebrews in chapter 11 tells us that the patriarch didn't even consider his old country as he did not want to be tempted to go back. As we continue in 2 Chronicles, look at the statement David makes:

*And David said to Solomon: "My son, as for me, it was in my mind to build a house to the name of the LORD my God."*

In order to be tempted by something, you must first be dwelling on it. If your mind is not focused on sin or secular things, Satan cannot entice you to partake in those things, and you will be completely open to the voice and call of God in your life. You will disarm the enemy completely. If you want to win any battle, the first step is taking captive your thoughts.

It is one thing to set yourself up for success with positive thinking, but in order to truly "make up your mind," you must become a person of declaration. When someone is dead set and fully confident of something, it is not only in their thoughts and dreams, but it is also in their speech. Think about your favorite food, sports team, or model of car. People will know that you are a San Diego Chargers fan by your constant confession of devotion for your team. People will know you are a Chevy, not a Ford, guy by your declaration (maybe even course jokes). By declaring things, you establish your personal culture. More importantly, by declaring truth over your identity, circumstances, and dreams you will fortify your stance and live with a mind that is set, focused, and made up.

Take for example this thought: I know without a shadow of doubt I will never get a divorce. People will warn you to "never say never." Some will reason, "even pastors fail and fall." I choose not to receive that. I have made up my mind. If you go into a commitment without a mind that is made up, you are setting yourself for open attack and vulnerability. However, if you take a stance, make up your mind, and declare truth over your marriage, it will not only last but thrive.

## *Operating from Rest*

A few years ago my church was in a tough financial bind. There was absolutely nothing in the bank account. There was no money to pay the bills or payroll. My pastor called a board meeting and presenting the issue. As they went to prayer to seek God's command and help, the Spirit spoke to my pastor and said to give money away. This is obviously radical and crazy, yet the entire board had the same stirring. The only problem was that there was no money to give away! As they trusted God, they wrote a check and blessed a sister church. That same day a random check was given to our church in the exact amount that we gave away. Our pastor decided to *trust* God and live by the promises God had given us. We are continuing to see God's provision in all areas of the church.

The greatest season that Israel ever experienced was led by a king who was at rest. Solomon trusted the Lord and leaned upon His wisdom to lead the Israelites. God brought increase, and favor was manifested throughout the people and land.

*Behold, a son shall be born to you, who shall be a man of rest; and I will give him rest from all his enemies all around. His name shall be Solomon, for I will give peace and quietness to Israel in his days. He shall build a house for My name.*

Matthew 6:27 says, "Which of you by worrying can add one cubit to his statue?" Nothing is accomplished by worrying. Worry will move you backward while worship will catapult you forward. You will find yourself stressed and worrying when you are under the false burden that you must fix your own problems based on your efforts and intelligence. You will become a person of rest when you can fully trust God and hold Him to His promises for your life and circumstances. No formula can teach you the lesson of trust; it is a quality one must gain in relationship with God. You must be convinced of God's ability and provision. You must be confident of His power and grandeur. When we are fearful of something, it is largely due to the fact that we are believing a lie that our issue is bigger than our God.

## Have an Encounter

You cannot operate in the kingdom if you are ignorant of the king. It is one thing to know *of* God and another thing entirely to be known *by* the Lord. The bridge from information to revelation is application. We cannot simply meet with God to receive information; we must encounter Him. Putting your faith to your feet is one of the greatest open doors to an encounter with God. Think back at a retreat, missions trip, or outreach you were a part of. Why is it that you feel so close to God and so in tune with His voice immediately after a church event or outreach? In my opinion it is because you *did something* for and with the Lord. When you take a risk and come into alignment with God's Word, your soul is awakened and you come alive.

David charged Solomon by saying

*Now, my son, may the LORD be with you; and may you prosper, and build the house of the LORD your God, as He has said to you. Only may the LORD give you wisdom and understanding.*

David told his son that it is not enough to simply have knowledge of God; he must also have understanding. There are moments when the promises of God become real and tangible. I remember as a teenager one night I was in bed late at night unable to fall asleep. I was battling a season of loneliness and loss of identity. I had been a Christian for a couple of years at this point and knew of God's love and provision, but that night a deep void and hurt were the center of my focus. At one point I couldn't even remain still. I finally sat up, moved over to the edge of the bed. With slumped shoulders and head down, I uttered, "God." In the second I said the name of God, a warmth rushed over me and I literally felt as if arms were around me. I was not crazy, nor was I half-asleep. I was literally embraced. In that moment I went from *knowing* God's love to *encountering* His love for me.

## *Permission to Be Like Jesus*

The Jewish people expected the Messiah to come to earth as a dominating King saving them from the oppressive kingdom of the Roman Empire. Jesus came to earth and did just that, but not in the aggressive manner they imagined. He brought so much more than just overtaking one government. He brought the government of heaven, which is family and power. He modeled how to keep our eyes focused on what the Father desired and not only healed diseases and performed miracles, but also commissioned His disciples and us to accomplish the same things.

Jesus said in John 14:12, "Most assuredly I say to you, he who believes in Me, the works that I do he will do also; and greater works than these he will do." This is a powerful verse and challenge to the believer. Jesus healed sickness, raised the dead, and cast out demons. He says in this verse that we are not only called to do those things, but *greater*. One thing I am certain of, I must do the things Jesus commanded me to do. I cannot do the things He did as God. I will not try to forgive people's sins, claim to be God, or receive worship, but I will, through His power, set out to accomplish the impossible and live supernaturally.

I cannot accept defeat, lack, sorrow, or powerlessness in my life when I claim to have God Himself living in my heart and possess freedom from all my sin. Jesus did away with the hindrances of sin. He purchased our pain and sickness so we wouldn't live in worry. The book of James chapter 1 states that if I lack wisdom, I can ask God, who gives it liberally. I am completely without excuse to live the abundant and overcoming life called the Christian faith. Bottom line, if Jesus did it and gave us permission to follow suit, I have the responsibility to do it.

# Chapter 2

## *Daddy Issues*

HE SLEPT SO STILL AND SO peacefully, it was almost as if he weren't breathing. The room was dimly lit and quiet; only the gently hum of the air-conditioning unit could be heard at three in the morning. The busy street directly outside our one-bedroom apartment was calm and almost deserted. I lay at the edge of the bed literally inches away from my newborn son, who was carefully swaddled in his bassinette. It was his first night home from the hospital, and the nerves of a first-time father would only allow me thirty minutes of sleep that night.

I never knew that a tiny and squirmy eight-pound, six-ounce baby could have such an incredible impact on my life. Before my son, I had never changed a diaper, prepared a bottle, or even held a baby. My boy was the first infant I had ever held, and I was literally so scared, it took my two full days after he was born to muster up the courage to even pick him up. On top of this already eventful time in my life, my wife had an emergency C-section, and the doctors had informed me that she was to be on complete bed rest for the next two weeks. This left an inexperienced and scared father to do all the caretaking of a new human life. It was literally the event I mark as turning me into a man.

We eventually adjusted to life as a family, and my son quickly caught on to sleeping through the night. Very soon after my son was born, we moved into a larger two-bedroom apartment in a better part of town. One night when he was about one and a half years old, he began crying around two in the morning. My wife and were used to him occasionally waking up letting out a small cry but drifting back to sleep soon thereafter. As he cried, my wife and I continued to lie in bed not wanting to rush in, and allow him to expect us to answer every single cry. This cry, however, was different. First off, he cried longer than he usually did. Then his cry turned into an exhausted whimper. I knew something was wrong, so I got up to check on my son. When I turned on the light, he was not in his crib. Any parent will know what I felt at that moment. It is when all the blood in your body flushes warm, everything in the world stops, and a spirit of dread overtakes you.

I ran to the crib and found my son wedged between the mattress frame and the sliding front gate. Months of him jumping, shaking, and playing had loosened up the bolts of the crib, allowing him to roll over in the middle of the night and fall through the sliding front gate and the frame ultimately getting stuck at the head and unable to move. He was half-asleep, exhausted from crying and pain. Every muscle in my body seemed to flood with adrenaline in that moment, and I literally ripped the gate clear off the frame. I freed my son, held him close, and placed my hand over the red mark on the side of his face. By this time, my wife had heard all the commotion and ran into the room. She took our son into our bed, and I stayed behind to have a little "talk" with that crib.

In those early morning hours on that day, I did what any loving parent would do. As a father I have the responsibility to love, care for, and guide my son. Unfortunately in our society today, not everyone has had a wonderful experience with their father. Your father may have abandoned you. Maybe he was there in your home but wasn't really "there." Some fathers wind up in deep addictions and some go to the lengths of abusing the very children they are supposed to love. It is no secret that we need a revival of godly men in our nation and the world. A broken home can hold a believer back from their destiny if they allow it to. I am convinced that God can restore and reconcile and family issue or pain, despite the offense or crime. Despite what your experience was growing up with your earthly father, we must never let it taint the truth of who our Heavenly Father is to us.

It is so critically important how we view and think about God…it is so critically important how we view and think about God. Your perspective of God will determine your intimacy with Him. In the same way an unhealthy earthly relationship will cause separation, so will an unhealthy spiritual relationship keep you separated from the Father. God will "never leave us or forsake us," yet our *awareness* of Him can dissolve and we can walk this life completely ignoring the Father if our perspective of Him is polluted by the enemy and the world.

## *God Is Good*

History, tradition, and Hollywood have painted a wrong idea of who God the Father is. He is not a Zeus-like being that watches every move of man, waiting to strike every failure with lightning bolts. God is not a calloused, hardened, and stoic old man that sits on a golden throne with lowered eyebrows. The Bible says in Psalm 2:4, "He who sits in the heavens shall laugh." God's nature and core are love and goodness. Take a glance at how the account of Matthew chapter 7 puts it:

*Ask and it will be given to you; seek and you will find; knock and the door will be opened to you. For everyone who asks receives; he who seeks finds; and to him who knocks, the door will be opened. Which of you, if his son asks for bread, will give him a stone? Or if he asks for a fish, will give him a snake? If you, then, though you are evil, know how to give good gifts to your children, how much more will your Father in heaven give good gifts to those who ask him!*

The Bible here is basically saying that if *you* know how to be a loving and good parent, don't you think Almighty God can be far greater of a parent than you? Our culture has been polluted with ideas and thoughts that God brings sickness in our lives to teach us different lessons, that the Lord is angry with us all the time unless we walk in perfect obedience. Simply because God created the world and holds the universe in His hands, He is blamed for every tragedy, hurt, and sickness. It is very similar to something I learned during my time as a youth pastor. I came to find out that whatever happens on youth night, whether good or bad, the next morning, it is always the youth pastor's fault! I may not have been the one who broke the window, but because I am in charge, it is my fault. We have to stop blaming God for the things in this world that are a result of sin and the evil one.

Again, the very nature of God is good and loving. Many believers today have not found their way out of the Old Testament. Though we still gain powerful truth from the old covenant, we must remember that we are under grace, not the law or condemnation. The Bible says in Romans 8:1, "*There is* therefore now no condemnation to those who are in Christ Jesus." We see incredible things in the Old Testament that cause us to believe God is an angry god who must seek judgment.

Accounts like the flood in Genesis 6 or Sodom and Gomorrah in Genesis 19 have been burned into the memory of our hearts that God is out to get us if we don't behave. Yes, it is true that sin must be punished, and we see this in the Old Testament, but we must never forget that *all* our sins, past, present, and future, were already punished on a cross two thousand years ago. God sees us through the lens of the blood of His son.

You can still see the reminiscences of Old Testament thinking whenever a tragedy or natural disaster happens in our nation. I remember when Hurricane Katrina literally wiped out New Orleans, people began claiming that God was judging that city. I even heard one pastor comment (I wish not to mention his name) that when "sin abounds, God's hand of protection is lifted." In my opinion, if something awful happens as a result of sin, the blame is the sin, not God! The Gospel of John says in chapter 10:

> *The thief does not come except to steal, and to kill,*
> *and to destroy. I have come that they may have life,*
> *and that they may have it more abundantly.*

Satan is to blame for all the evil that we see in this world. We need to stop pointing the finger at God and accusing Him of doing nothing when He has equipped us completely to destroy the works of the enemy here on earth. I've heard it said that we need to "stop putting the responsibility on God that He gave us authority to handle."

It is absolutely critical that we view God as on our side and for us. The view we have of God will tremendously affect how we love and receive from Him. Take a look at account of those in Jesus' hometown from Mark chapter 6:

> *And they took offense at him. Jesus said to them, "Only in his hometown, among his relatives and in his own house is a prophet without honor." He could not do any miracles there, except lay his hands on a few sick people and heal them.*

Jesus grew up a typical Jewish boy, studying the Torah and eventually taking on the family business of carpentry. They saw this Jesus they had grown up with performing miracles, preaching the kingdom of God, and healing the sick. But because they *knew* Him, they took *offense* at Him. They gave Jesus no honor, and because of a lack of faith or belief in what He could do, they were left without a touch from God. Yes, your perspective of God will affect how you commune and receive from Him.

Before my wife and I got married, she had purchased a Toyota Tacoma Prerunner, cool truck for a girl (Chevrolet Silverados are for men). She borrowed money from a family member and made monthly payments to pay back the debt. When we got married, we sold that truck and had about five hundred dollars left to pay off the balance. Since we were newly married, money was not at an all-time high. It took us a solid two years to pay that small balance. In the time it took us to pay the funds back, this family member stopped sending birthday cards and started sending notes about paying the balance in a timely manner. Our relative was offended, so were we, and the outcome was separation. We (in sin) based our view of this relative with bitterness and complaint. We were upset that there was such a demand from a person who was financially stable and for such a small amount.

Our perspective caused us to incorrectly label someone, and the result was separation and no communication.

From an early age we are taught the wrong ways to approach relationships and trouble. When we don't get along with someone, we separate ourselves from that person. You may have experienced this in your family growing up. Maybe your father was angry with your uncle over something small and the result was you not being able to see your uncle for a while, possibly years because Dad was angry with him. Think about when you got in trouble as a kid. Typically if you did something wrong, the outcome was your mom or dad sending you to your room until you could behave. They would separate themselves from you because of *your behavior* and not come close to you again until you would behave better.

## *God Loves You*

A while back, our worship team was leading the church in the John Mark McMillan song "He Loves Me." We went into an extended period of time singing the lyrics, "He loves me, oh how He loves me!" Our pastor got up on the stage and said, "We all know how important it is to love God with all our hearts, but I don't think we understand how powerful it is to *know* that God loves you." We were led in a time of basking in the love of God. For many it was the first time they had seen God in this light. We forget at times that our relationship with God is two-way: we are to love Him, but we are also required to receive His love in return.

As I mentioned earlier, it is extremely important that you view God as a loving and giving Father because your view of God will affect how you commune with God. What is also important is what you believe about how God views *you*. Take a look at the account of Jesus's baptism and see if you notice a theme:

> *Then Jesus came from Galilee to the Jordan to be baptized by John. But John tried to deter him, saying, "I need to be baptized by you, and do you come to me?" Jesus replied, "Let it be so now; it is proper for us to do this to fulfill all righteousness." Then John consented. As soon as Jesus was baptized, he went up out of the water. At that moment heaven was opened, and he saw the Spirit of God descending like a dove and lighting on him. And a voice from heaven said, "This is my Son, whom I love; with him I am well pleased." (Matthew 3:13–17)*

Before Jesus was the miracle worker, before He was the traveling rabbi, and before He ever laid hands on a sick person, Jesus was a *son* who knew His purpose and that His Father loved Him. Matthew 3 says that God the Father was "well pleased" with Jesus before Jesus began His three-year ministry. This shows us that we must find our worth in God and from the truth of our identity as His children. It simply cannot be about our performance or works.

We have to understand from the very beginning that God truly loves us and is pleased with us apart from our behavior or works. We cannot earn God's love; it has always been a gift.

At age twelve in Luke chapter 2, during a festival, Jesus's earthly parents *left Jesus behind!* Can you imagine being responsible for the Messiah and leaving Him behind? Three days later they found Him conversing with teachers and amazing them with His wisdom. He said, "Didn't you know I had to be in my Father's House (or about my Father's business)?" From a very early age Jesus knew His purpose and that He was dearly loved by the Father.

## God Wants to Bless You

The statement "God wants to bless you" will drive some people crazy. For so long the role of the believer has been to suffer, to live poor, and to be counted as worthless. It is almost as if the worse off your life is, the holier you are and the more God is pleased with you. I simply see no truth in this. What type of witness is that to the world? Do you think an unbeliever who is successful in the world's eye will be drawn to a life of misery and poverty?

With a wrong view of humility and God's blessing, it is easy to see why many churches focus so much on performance, sin, guilt, and condemnation. Allow me to expand on the thought of receiving God's blessing for your life:

## 1. Jesus paid a high price for you.

*For you were bought at a price; therefore glorify God in your body and in your spirit, which are God's. (1 Corinthians 6:20)*

It is completely ludicrous to think that Jesus would get off His throne in heaven, make His way to this earth, be brutally killed, and conquer death so that we could live poor, defeated lives. Jesus came to free us of our sin, yes, but we must not stop there and think that sin was the only thing Jesus came to conquer (I will go into detail of what our salvation brought us in the next chapter). So many Christians get saved, receive forgiveness of their sins, but never move forward. We think that sin is the only thing we must focus on in this life. So much of our preaching is on sin, obedience, and doing more for God, but Romans 6:11 says, "Likewise you also, reckon yourselves to be dead indeed to sin, but alive to God in Christ Jesus our Lord." If we are dead to sin and if Jesus washed *all* our sins away, why must we continue to focus on it?!

Staying focused on your sin is a trap of the enemy. It is safe and comfortable to "battle with sin" rather than conquer it and move forward.

Another excuse believers offer up is that this life is here today and gone tomorrow. James 4:14 says, "For what *is* your life? It is even a vapor that appears for a little time and then vanishes away." Many reason that because this life is obsolete in comparison to eternity, it, therefore, has no meaning or significance. This type of reasoning is false and against scripture. Jesus commanded us to accomplish things while on earth:

> And Jesus came and spoke to them, saying, "All authority
> has been given to Me in heaven and on earth. Go therefore
> and make disciples of all the nations, baptizing them in
> the name of the Father and of the Son and of the Holy
> Spirit, teaching them to observe all things that I have
> commanded you; and lo, I am with you always, even to
> the end of the age." Amen. (Matthew 28:18–20)

Earth is the stepping stone into eternity. If we receive salvation while on earth, how much more should we be doing for the lost who have yet to find Jesus? We have a mission while on earth. We have things that need to be done while here. The kingdom of God must be expanded, and the Lord has given us the privilege and responsibility to do so.

When I gave my life to the Lord as a teenager, it was due to the fact that the friends I had that were saved had a joy, peace, and power source that I needed and wanted. What type of witness would we be if we were, defeated, broke, poor, and powerless? No unbeliever would want to give up their lifestyle and success to step into the life of a defeated believer, even if we threaten them with burning in hell. There must be something about our lives that leads them to saving grace. The fact that the Holy Spirit lives within us should be enough to challenge us to reach higher levels and accomplish more. It is not wrong to think that because God Himself dwells within us and we have communication with Him, we should actually be doing *better* than the world that does not know or have access to God! Christians should be the smartest, richest, healthiest, and most peaceful people on the planet because we have a connection to the God who made it all.

## 2. If you have nothing, what can you give away?

There is a false humility that says, "If I have nothing, it means I have given all of myself and my resources to others." The problem with this mentality is that if you have given all you have away and do not expect God to bless you, what else can you possibly give? True prosperity is not how much you can get from God and hoard; it is measured by how much you are able to bless and give away. Second Corinthians 8:9 says, "For you know the grace of our Lord Jesus Christ, that though He was rich, yet for your sakes He became poor, that you through His poverty might become rich." The issue believers have is not in receiving wealth; the problem is managing it well. Many believers are automatically turned off to money or wealth because of the past abuses of others in the faith. We can't let others' mistakes compromise what God says is true, nor can we misuse God's wealth to us by keeping it.

Some people misquote scripture and say, "Money is the root of all evil." The truth is found in 1 Timothy 6:10, which says, "For the *love* of money is the root of all kinds of evil [italics mine]." Money has taken a bad rap in the Christian world, but the truth is that we need money for certain things. We need money to fund missionaries in Africa; we need money to pay bills, cover college tuition, etc. I have gotten into lengthy debates over money, wealth, and blessing, but it all boils down to the fact that if you have nothing, how can you give? God wants us to be lenders, not borrowers. We, as believers, need to be positioned to be a blessing unto others.

## Go

Before God created this universe, there was *heaven*. Jesus came from *heaven* to earth, and in the end we will see a new *heaven* descend to a new earth (Revelation 21:1). It seems in the grand scheme of things, the realities of heaven have been the will of the Father. God desires that none would perish but that all would come to salvation (2 Peter 3:9). It is safe to say that God desires relationship with us, that he desires to bless us, and that as a loving Father, He wants the best for us. We know that in heaven there is no sorrow, sickness, or sin. I believe God's heart is to see these realities alive, even in this world, through the blood of His son. Let me expand this thought with these scriptures:

*For our citizenship is in heaven, from which we also eagerly wait for the Savior, the Lord Jesus Christ. (Philippians 3:20)*

*Which He worked in Christ when He raised Him from the dead and seated Him at His right hand in the heavenly places. (Ephesians 1:20)*

As citizens of heaven, we are commissioned and positioned in this land to bring in the kingdom of Heaven. Jesus prayed this in Matthew 6:10, "Your kingdom come. Your will be done on earth as *it is* in heaven." Though God is all-powerful, He is in the business of using people like you and me to carry out His desire and will for this world and beyond. First Corinthians 3:9 says it beautifully, "For we are God's fellow workers; you are God's field, *you are* God's building."

God created this great and wonderful world but placed a man, Adam, to have dominion over it. God established a covenant of the law but used a man, Moses, to release it. Even Jesus came in the form of both God and *man* into this world to redeem it and carry out the Father's will. God is in the business of using people to carry out the desires of His heart. We as His beloved children must be willing to heed His call and carry out His desires.

# Chapter 3

## *Unwrapping the Gift*

ONE DAY WHILE WAITING AT a traffic light, I noticed a brand-new Corvette pulling up on my right side. As the car came into better focus in my rearview mirror, I could instantly tell that this was no ordinary Corvette. It was in fact, a brand-new Z06. If you are unaware of this car, let me break it down for you. The Z06 is powered by an LS7 seven-liter V-8 that pushes 505 horsepower. It has a top racetrack-tested speed of 198 miles per hour.[1] This car can literally hit 90 miles an hour in second gear! Every detail of this car is built for speed, including the pressurized oil that keeps every mechanical part protected, even under high speeds and stress.

I was in awe of the power that was creeping up next to me, but then I saw something more shocking—a handicap placard on the rearview mirror and a little white-haired lady barely able to look over the steering wheel. No offense to my elderly friends, but let's be honest; I don't think Grandma is going to hit 198 miles per hour anytime soon! My joy turned into a mild sadness as I mourned the fact that this poor Corvette would never reach its full potential.

You and I, much like that Corvette, have been geared for greatness. Jesus came to this earth to set us free from our sin,

---

1    http://www.chevrolet.com/corvette-z06/#performance

sickness, bondage, and poverty with His death on the cross and resurrection from the grave. Not only did He take a huge weight off our shoulders, but He also blessed us and *gave to us* everything we will ever need in life. He gave us the Holy Spirit upon salvation (Luke 11:13), God has given us "every Spiritual blessing" (Ephesians 1:3), and He removed our struggle against the devil (1 John 3:8). But like the elderly lady in the Corvette, we have barely tapped into all that God has given to us. The Greek word for salvation is *sótéria*, which means, "welfare, prosperity, deliverance, preservation, salvation, safety."[2] It is safe to say that we are barely walking in a fourth of our salvation. While it is easy to receive the forgiveness of our sins, many believers do not walk in the reality that their sickness, poverty, and despair were also conquered on the cross. I would like to unwrap the gift of salvation with scripture, but first I feel I must set it up by quickly explaining the difference between the old and new covenants.

## The Old Has Gone; the New Has Come

Adam and Eve violated the one and only commandment that God gave them. He gave them the entire world to rule and take from, yet they broke the one rule He gave them. With this act of rebellion, sin entered the world. The Bible says that the "wages of sin is death" (Romans 6:23). God didn't stop Adam and Eve from making the mistake because God made people and not robots. God loves us unconditionally, but He desires that we love Him by our choice. If we were forced to love God, it wouldn't be love. Free will allowed Adam and Eve to sin, thus letting sin and the consequence of sin into the world.

---

2    http://concordances.org/greek/4991.htm

In a symbolic sense God gave Adam and Eve "the keys of the kingdom." When they sinned, they handed over the keys to Satan. It is no surprise that in the very next chapter in Genesis, we see the first murder taking place. Sin made its way into the world, and a long history of pain, rebellion, and destruction had begun.

In the first chapter of Job, we see God questioning Satan as to where he had been:

> *One day the angels came to present themselves before the LORD, and Satan also came with them. The LORD said to Satan, "Where have you come from?" Satan answered the LORD, "From roaming through the earth and going back and forth in it." (Job 1:6–7)*

Satan, "the prince of the world," now had his rule and was causing pain throughout the land. The wages of sin brought about not only death but also separation from God. Only obedience and righteousness gave man an opportunity to commune with God. Man lived in covenant with God, as we have seen with the patriarchs Abraham, Isaac, Jacob, and Joseph. Yet when man stumbled and failed, there was condemnation and separation.

Moses in Exodus 20 brought the nation of Israel, God's chosen people, the Ten Commandments. Moses also brought the law in which if you followed, you would be blessed, and if you broke, you would be cursed. The idea seemed good. If you do what is right, you would be blessed. The problem is that man is fallen and sin was in the world, making the law simply impossible to follow.

*For whoever keeps the whole law and yet stumbles at just
one point is guilty of breaking all of it. (James 2:10)*

It is almost frustrating to read the history of the Israelites in the Old Testament. It was a dramatic roller-coaster ride of obedience and rebellion. It was extremely clear that the world was in desperate need of a Savior.

## *Jesus the Savior*

*Now this is eternal life: that they may know you, the only true
God, and Jesus Christ, whom you have sent. —John 17:3*

Salvation is believing Jesus as Savior, confessing Him as Lord, and receiving what He died for. Romans 10:9 says "that if you confess with your mouth the Lord Jesus and believe in your heart that God has raised Him from the dead, you will be saved." It is a complete gift to us, something that we did not and cannot earn through our own merit or works. The Bible makes it clear that Jesus is the only way to the Father and Heaven:

*Jesus said to him, "I am the way, the truth, and the life. No
one comes to the Father except through Me." (John 14:6)*

Though this information may seem elementary and simple, it is true and often overlooked. We may know that Jesus died for us, but in the midst of circumstances we tend to focus on our own problems and attempt to work out our issues through our own strength and intelligence. In a sense we are trying to be our own savior. If Jesus was the one that died for anything we will ever face in life, He should be the first person and help we go to.

## More Than Just a Ticket to Heaven

The Bible says in Hosea 4:6, "My people are destroyed for lack of knowledge." If you don't know what you have, you can't use or operate it. On the other hand, you may know what you have, yet never "open" it. One of the greatest joys I have is blessing my son with surprises and gifts. I love Christmases and birthdays because I get to be a part of bringing so much joy to the face and heart of my son. It would be odd and alarming to give my son a gift and for him to reject it, saying, "No, thank you." Yet this is what we do every day. God has given us a gift and His children give a polite "No, thank you." Allow me to walk you through all that Jesus promised and gave to you.

## Peace

*Peace I leave with you. My peace I give to you; not as the world gives do I give to you. Let not your hearts be troubled, neither let it be afraid. — John 14:27*

A few months ago I was in the front row of my church, listening to my pastor's sermon, when I felt a tap on my shoulder. An usher went over and whispered in my ear, "You are needed in the cry room." So I stood up and made my way over to the little room off the side of the sanctuary where nursing mothers take crying babies in the middle of service. I was a bit confused as to why I was needed in the cry room, but the request seemed urgent.

When I entered the room, there was a mother, a son (about twenty years old), and another pastor on staff. This kid looked as if he had been pummeled by a street gang, and you could tell he was in a fight for his soul.

I asked what the problem was, and the pastor explained to me that this young man was under an attack of the enemy and wanted freedom. I looked at this young man with authority and boldness and began asking him a series of questions. I asked if he had received Jesus as his savior (in which he had), I asked if he wanted complete freedom (he nodded yes), and finally I asked him if he *believed* that God was able to set him free completely and permanently (he said yes). After the questions, all I did was repeat scripture after scripture of what God had given to him and who he was in Christ. I didn't shout, scream, or go to "war with the devil." If this young man knew Jesus, then he had everything he needed for complete and lasting victory.

Once I laid the groundwork of fortifying his identity and renewing his mind with the truth of God's Word, I prayed a simple and calm prayer for the peace of God to fill his life. The second I said *peace*, he dropped to the floor and began growling but very soon after was completely released of any and all demonic oppression. God's peace is a strong and powerful weapon.

You can walk in complete peace when your mind is in agreement with the truth of God's Word and what He says about you. You and I have the privilege of growing in a *relationship* with God. We are the ones responsible to become more aware of Him in our lives and grow in our understanding of His ways. When our hearts are for the Lord, we begin to develop a history with God. Creating memories with friends and family is a blessing, yet with the Lord it is critical. When you have a history with God, it allows you to look back and remember, "If He got me through *that*, He will get me through *this*."

## *Healing*

*Who Himself bore our sins in His own body on the tree, that we, having died to sins, might live for the righteousness—by whose stripes you were healed. —1 Peter 2:24*

A few years ago our staff here at my church went to a conference in Camarillo, California, that was really a workshop for how to heal the sick. Together we pastors spent four days learning what the Bible says on healing and discovering that we could pray for the sick and expect to see them healed by the authority God has given us (I go into greater detail of our authority in the next chapter). One day after one of the workshops, my pastor, our children's pastor, and myself were up in our hotel and were wanting to test out what we just learned. My pastor asked if any of us were sick in any way so we could practice praying. None of us were sick, but I remember that I was deaf in my left ear.

As a kid I had a multitude of troubles in my ears. I developed a disease I cannot pronounce. It basically ate away at my eardrum and shattered the three hearing bones located in the middle ear. I could hear at about 5 percent in my left ear. We decided we would practice praying by praying for my hearing to be restored. As we went through the checklist of what we needed to do, my pastor asked if I had ever spoken a vow over my ear. I said yes. For the longest time, to ensure that people would speak into my good ear, I would say, "I'm deaf in the left." So I broke the vow, and the pastors quickly prayed for me. When they had finished, they asked if I could do something I couldn't do before. I responded by saying, "My doctor would snap his fingers in front of my ears so that I could test out the difference." When I snapped my fingers across my ears, I was shocked to discover I had perfect hearing in both ears.

Many Christians believe that God can heal them but do not expect for God to heal them on a daily basis. Most believe you have to be "lucky" enough or become some type of super-Christian in order to receive the miraculous. We have forgotten that healing is part of the salvation package even prophesied years before Jesus was even born:

*But he was pierced for our transgressions, he was crushed for our iniquities; the punishment that brought us peace was upon him, and by his wounds we are healed. (Isaiah 53:5)*

I am simply convinced of divine health, again, because if there is no sickness in heaven, I should not expect it in my life. I choose to stand upon the truth of the word and not accept sickness or disease in my life or in my home.

While on earth, Jesus preached the Good News, cast out demons, and healed sicknesses. He not only paved the way so we could experience freedom, health, and joy, but He has also equipped us to do the same:

*Very truly I tell you, whoever believes in Me will do the works I have been doing, and they will do even greater things than these. (John 14:12)*

*Heal the sick, cleanse the lepers, raise the dead, cast out demons.*
*Freely you have received, freely give. (Matthew 10:8)*

## Provision

*For you know the grace of our Lord Jesus Christ, that though He*
*was rich, yet for your sakes became poor, that you through His*
*poverty might become rich. —2 Corinthians 8:9*

There are many topics that are highly debated among
Christians. Prosperity is one of those hot buttons. When we
think of prosperity, we automatically think about the television
evangelists who have hundreds of thousands of dollar salaries
and fly around in private jets. We revert to the cheesiness of
preachers on TV who claim you can have power, victory, and
healing for only $19.99 and a bottle of miracle water. Our view
of godly prosperity has been polluted again by the media and
gossip. We must remember that prosperity is more than just
money. As children of God we are to *prosper* in all areas of our
lives, be it relationships, workplaces, businesses, and finances.
Let me also say that not every TV preacher is a greedy partner
of the devil. Many of these preachers made an abundance of
money through book sales, speaking engagements, and products.
There is nothing wrong with being blessed through good, old-
fashioned hard work. Many of these preachers give away just as
much as they received and are good stewards of the blessing God
has given.

As we view our lives, including prosperity through *Heaven-*
*Colored Sunglasses*, we are reminded again that if we have the
most powerful Being in the universe in our lives, we should
expect to be well taken care of. If my God can conquer the grave

and all the power of hell, He can bless me with enough resource and blessing that I am taken care of and can be a channel of blessing myself.

This concept is foreign in the church as we have been conditioned to think, "Sacrifice as much as you can, live off as little as you can for the benefit of others." Let me use the example of overseas missions again. I have heard the argument that it is absolutely wrong to have a nice house, cars that work properly, and a savings account when there are starving children all around the world. Condemnation is placed on believers if we are not living in poverty for the benefit of others. Again my response is simple, "If you have nothing, how do you plan to give?" You can empty your savings account, sell all your possessions, and give everything away, but how do you expect to *keep* blessing people once all you things are gone? God wants to bless us so that we can be a blessing. If I am financially set, I will always have room to give financially to those who are in need. Now, let me just throw out a disclaimer. I don't feel there is a need for believers to drive around in exotic $250,000 cars and tens of thousands of dollars' worth in jewelry. I don't feel there is a need for nonbelievers to ride around in exotic $250,000 cars! All these material things will pass. I do feel, however, that we should be able to have cars that are paid off, that are *safe*, and that won't break down on us. I believe we should have homes that are large enough to accommodate our families and visitors. God wants to bless us, and we are called to bless others.

A wonderful example of this is a story I heard about Rick Warren, pastor at Saddleback Church and author of *The Purpose Driven Life*. Pastor Warren has sold millions of copies of his book and double that in all the resources from it. He is extremely well-off financially. He has a lovely home, I would assume. He has a nice car and money to bless his family. But what I hear is that he is a reverse tither, meaning he gives 90 percent of his income to God and lives off 10 percent. At a conference I went to years ago, Pastor Warren said he has paid back Saddleback church every cent they had ever given him in salary. This is a wonderful example of stewarding well the blessing of God.

## Deliverance

*For this purpose the Son of God was manifested that He might destroy the works of the devil.* —1 John 3:8b

If there is one major area in life where we need to view things through *heaven-colored sunglasses*, it is in the area of spiritual warfare (more on this in chapter 5). The Bible says in Romans 16:20 that Jesus "will crush Satan under our feet." When Jesus died on a cross, He defeated the power of darkness completely and eternally. The only way the devil has power over your life is when you come into agreement with him, much like Adam and Eve did. When we are saved by the blood of Jesus, we literally become invincible to the dark forces. Not to say that we won't be oppressed by the devil, persecuted, or troubled in this world. The Bible says in John 16:33, "These things I have spoken to you, that in Me you may have peace. In the world you will have tribulation; but be of good cheer, I have overcome the world." It is true that we will all face trials and hurt in this life, but nowhere do I see that we as believers are supposed to *stay* there! It is safe to say that one believer with a renewed mind is more powerful than all hell combined.

## Releasing God's Power

The devil has tried to take me out from ministry on a couple occasions. I remember after working at my first church for seven years, I was let go and replaced by a more experienced youth pastor. This left me hurt and bitter, and I vowed I would never enter into ministry again. I began interviewing at every nonministry business possible and even making it into a few second interviews, but I wasn't getting hired anywhere. With a three-month-old baby and a family to take care of, I was running out of options. Our credit cards were maxed, and it was a miracle we were surviving. I finally got to a point where I sat down with God and said, "All right, Lord, I will call one church and one church only. If they have something available for me, I will take it." My wife had gotten saved at a local church in town, so I decided I would try that church. I found the number online and called. A receptionist picked up, and I said, "Random question, but do you have any employment opportunities at your church?" She asked me what my experience was. I responded by saying, "I have down everything from maintenance to administration to youth ministry." She interrupted me and said, "You know, we are hiring a youth pastor and we haven't even advertised it." The rest is history.

I have seen the Lord perform miracle after miracle like this in so many ways, and each time the miracle was released when I came into alignment with my true identity and the promises of His Word. The most powerful and life-changing truth in our faith is renewing your mind.

*And do not be conformed to this world, but be transformed by the renewing of your mind, that you may prove what is that good and acceptable and perfect will of God.—Romans 12:2*

## Stay Focused on Truth

There are many helpful things you can do to keep your mind renewed and your life held in agreement with the promises and Word of God.

### 1. We must become Bible literate

*Jesus answered and said to them, "You are mistaken, not knowing the Scriptures nor the power of God." (Matthew 22:29)*

*And that from childhood you have known the Holy Scriptures, which are able to make you wise for salvation through faith which is in Christ Jesus. (2 Timothy 3:15)*

Taking time to regularly study Scripture is more than just a discipline that is commanded of us (Joshua 1:8, Psalm 1:3). It is the truth that must become our lifestyle so that we can release the power of God into our lives. You cannot release what you don't have or know. Your identity is also shaped by your understanding of the Word of God. How will you know who you are if you never take the time to study what God has said about you?

One discipline that I do is to create a list of scripture that speaks life to my circumstances. If you are battling depression, find every scripture you can on joy and peace and declare them over your life. If you are dealing with a season of lack, find every scripture on prosperity and provision and declare them. You are the only one responsible for renewing your mind.

## 2. Remember your testimonies

As I mentioned earlier, when you remember what God has done for you, you can say to yourself, "He got me through *that* and He will get me through *this*." Reflecting on the positive things the Lord has done in your life will build a confidence in your heart and a strong trust in the Lord. We cannot afford to make our problems bigger than our God.

## *Don't Be Fooled*

A few years ago there was a TV show that came on called *Magic: Secrets Finally Revealed*. The program was about a host magician who masked himself all season long, uncovering the secrets behind the world's most famous illusions and magic tricks. We saw many of Houdini's famous death-defying illusions and how they were done. We saw the secret behind sawing a woman in half and even how to make an airplane disappear. Though the show was intriguing, it was also depressing. It took all the fun out of "magic" and made you feel almost ripped off. The magician, who revealed his identity at the end, created the show as a challenge to magicians to come up with better and more elaborate tricks and illusions.

The enemy today is trying to do the same thing. We are faced with all kinds of issues, problems, hurts, and worries in life, but every single thing that you and I will ever face was conquered on the cross. We may feel overwhelmed and underqualified, yet Christ came to set us free from all bondages and purchase all that we would ever need for a life of complete and lasting victory and success.

# Chapter 4

## *The Ball Is in Your Court*

THE ALTAR TEAM WAS IN place and ministering as people came forward for prayer while most of the congregation trickled out of the last service of the day. I was in the front row with my wife and went up to compliment our pastor on the sermon. He put his hand on my shoulder and asked, "So has the Lord placed anything on your heart for tonight?"

April 3, 2011, will be a day I will never forget. It was the first time our church had ever put on a healing service. Though we had been walking in the power of God and had the faith to the heal the sick for years, this was the first time we had taken a risk, opened an event to the public, and welcomed all who were sick, diseased, or terminally ill to go for healing. In response to my pastor's question, I said, "I know that God has said that we must go after the most difficult case right at the beginning." And that's exactly what we did.

There was an anticipation in the air like I have never seen. It felt as if everyone in the church were expecting the miraculous, and you could almost feel the unity in the air. Most of the church staff spent the time between the last morning service and the 6:00 PM healing service in prayer and fasting to simply prepare our hearts and create a greater sensitivity to the Spirit.

The worship team opened up with the first song in what felt like a standing room only. I went on stage to take the risk the Lord had spoken to me about earlier. I took the microphone and said, "Tonight we have come to agree with heaven and witness the miraculous." I went on to ask, "Do we believe God is able?" and the church enthusiastically responded with "Amen!" I again asked, "Is God bigger than anything we could ever face?" Louder the church said, "Amen!" I then proceeded to announce, "Then we are not going to wait until after the worship music or even after the sermon to heal the sick. I feel as if God wants to heal the most difficult case in the room right now!" You could see heads turning all around and a hush come over the church as everyone waited to see who would dare volunteer.

Coming down the left aisle was a middle-aged man who held the hand of a nine-year-old boy. When he got to the front of the stage, I asked, "What is it we can pray for?" The man (the child's grandfather) explained that the boy had a condition that left him blind in one eye and was losing sight in the other. He had had a fever of 104 degrees for over six days. The doctors could not do anything, and the boy's mother didn't even want the child to leave the house—even if it was a "healing night." She gave specific instructions to take the child to the church, get him prayed for, and take him right back. The grandfather thanked the mother and in mighty faith brought his grandchild to the church. When he heard the invitation at the beginning of the service, he jumped at the opportunity.

The church extended their hands forward; I placed my hand on the child's head and began to pray. Afterward, we all applauded and pressed in to see if God had answered our prayer. We had the child cover his good eye and attempt to tell us how many fingers he could see us holding up. At about ten feet away, my pastor held up two fingers, and the boy, without hesitation, said, "Two." The church . . . exploded!

We tested him again, this time moving farther and farther away each time, and he nailed every one of the tests. After following up with the grandpa, we learned that the fever instantly disappeared and he was able to stay for the whole service. The next day at a restaurant, the boy was able to read the entire menu, something he couldn't do before.

That was how the service began. We entered back into worship, and Pastor delivered a small sermon on the power of healing. We began to call out different sicknesses and conditions, and people were getting healed left and right. One man came forward for healing of Parkinson's disease. Everyone knew him as the man who walked with a shuffle and a hand close to his side at all times. As I prayed for him, he fell under the power of God and lay there for a while. As I went on to pray for other people, out of nowhere, he got up and began running around the sanctuary, completely healed. The faith in the room was electrifying, and people were getting healed, saved, and delivered without even getting prayed for. It was a night to remember, but in all honestly it was simply a normal day in normal Christianity.

## *All Authority in Heaven . . .*

The love of God is powerful. God in His great mercy has not only saved us from hell and showered us with blessing; He has removed the worry and fear of the plan and work of the enemy. God has not left us as orphans in a foreign world. When we welcomed Jesus into our hearts and lives, we were given permission and authority to operate in the dominion we were given from the creation of this world.

God, through the work of the cross, has set us up for lasting victory and tremendous peace:

*Now if we are children, then we are heirs—heirs of God and co-heirs with Christ, if indeed we share in his sufferings in order that we may also share in his glory. (Romans 8:17)*

We have an inheritance of God's love, power, and peace for this world. We, through the name of Jesus and power of God, have the ability to change our circumstances and refuse to live a miserable and defeated life. Allow me to expand on this thought with a passage from Matthew 12:

*While He was still talking to the multitudes, behold, His mother and brothers stood outside, seeking to speak with Him. Then one said to Him, "Look, Your mother and Your brothers are standing outside, seeking to speak with You." But He answered and said to the one who told Him, "Who is My mother and who are My brothers?" And He stretched out His hand toward His disciples and said, "Here are My mother and My brothers! For **whoever** does the will of My Father in heaven is My brother and sister and mother." (emphasis mine)*

We have already established that we, through Christ, are children of God. Jesus, in this passage, says, in a different light, that we are family with Jesus (mother, brother, sister). The only prerequisite is doing the "will of the Father." The Bible makes it clear in 2 Peter 3:9 that God is "not willing that any should perish but that all should come to repentance." God's desire is that we come to know Him through salvation, and salvation sets us up for power, victory, and the ability to spread His kingdom on earth.

Jesus gave powerful commandments and authority to his disciples, and because I consider myself family to God, I can interpret the commands Jesus gave to His disciples as my own. Some may disagree and say that the commandments and authority that Jesus gave to His disciples were solely for His disciples, not modern-day believers. The problem with accepting this belief is that you would have to toss out 90 percent of what Jesus said we could do from the New Testament. If only the disciples, specifically the twelve, were only allowed to perform miracles, what about the passage in Mark 9?

> *But Jesus said, "Do not forbid him, for no **one** who works a miracle in My name can soon afterward speak evil of Me. For he who is not against us is on our side." (emphasis mine)*

There were other people performing miracles in Jesus's name, and Jesus specifically allowed it if it was done in accordance with God's will and His name. There are other accounts of men and women in the Bible performing miracles that were not a part of the twelve disciples.

Another argument about our authority and the supernatural is that the purpose of the miraculous was intended to "jump-start" the first-century church and validate Jesus's ministry but that miracles, signs, and wonders passed after the apostles. I have yet to find a scripture that validates that claim. I have found scripture like the one in Matthew 7:22, which says the following:

*Many will say to Me in that day, "Lord, Lord, have we not prophesied in Your name, cast out demons in Your name, and done many wonders in Your name?"*

What this scripture says to me is that up until the last days, we will still be walking in power and signs and wonders. Though this particular scripture is focused on people who perform wonders yet did not *know* God. It still demonstrates that the miraculous is ongoing and has not ceased in the first century. We should not brush off the power of God and limit it only for a specific season in the first century. With over two thousand years of church history, we should be so much greater than the first church. Though the church in Acts should always serve as the original blueprint, it should never be something we hope to attain as a means of an end. We should be the living legacy of the first-century church in which we continue to grow and move from glory to glory.

The Bible has some bold statements about us, and the truth is that God will never force us into our destiny. When we read the scriptures for ourselves, we must be the ones that decide to take the step of faith, pursue the risk, and explore *all* that God has for us.

*As you go, preach this message: "The kingdom of heaven is near." Heal the sick, raise the dead, cleanse those who have leprosy, drive out demons. Freely you have received, freely give." (Matthew 10:8)*

Here we see Jesus giving us authority over sickness, death, disease, and demons. This commandment is extremely liberating and offers amazing encouragement. Understanding the authority we have in Christ gives us freedom, boldness, and confidence in this fallen world. We no longer have to stand as victims but can rise up as the victors that we are destined to be in this world. Because of the sacrifice Christ made for us, we have the power to change any and every circumstance in our lives.

People today are overloaded with information. Simply look at the advances in technology and the availability of information today compared to a hundred years ago. We have no problem finding information in our society, including religious information. What the world is crying out for is power, the real deal, and something worth living and dying for. Billions of people have a void in the heart because they are not even scratching the surface of their identities and destines and are looking for any experience or encounter to meet the need and fill the void. For this reason, the supernatural (demonic side), such as vampire movies, Harry Potter, and haunted places are so popular. People are craving something that goes outside of their realities, something that has power, and something that cannot be produced by a camera or computer. Satan has made himself readily available for all who desire such an encounter but at such a high price and with such destruction. Jesus provided a grave-conquering power to all who would come to Him. Unfortunately, people will not receive what Christ has died for unless they are told and *shown!* We have a responsibility to walk in our true authority and identity that the world may know there is a God in heaven who is bigger than anything you will ever face and can handle any problem you ever encounter.

I have seen dozens of people come into our church and have a dynamic encounter with God, get healed, or have someone give them a word and reads their mail and it births a commitment to the Lord and ministry like nothing else. Let me just say that what Jesus has done for us and the written Word of God are enough entirely to bring someone to saving grace. The preaching of the Word has accomplished the great commission and the will of God, but we have been given authority that the world may know God and that hope may arise!

A greater tragedy than the hurt and trials we face today is a person who has the ability and power to change those circumstances but fails to walk in victory due to ignorance, defiance, or apathy.

I cannot imagine where my life would be today had I not come into the revelation of what He has done for me. Everything from my marriage to my finances to my ministry would be laced with worry, fear, insecurity, and stress. Stepping into truth has given me lasting victory and a boldness to proclaim the truth of God. I have no fears or worries knowing that my God has provided for me and has equipped me as a world changer.

## Unrestricted Kingdom Power

It is a wonderful joy to discover every day what God has done for us and said about us. However, we still continue to live in a foreign kingdom called earth. While we live and operate in this kingdom, we must continue to live uninfluenced by the world and see through *heaven-colored sunglasses*. We have been given an assignment in this world and a command from God to create a collision with this world and God's kingdom. This requires discipline as there are a million voices screaming for our attention and influences that bombard us on a daily basis, if not moment by moment. I want to walk through the sixth chapter of the book of Mark to highlight clear examples of how Jesus set the disciples up with kingdom power while living in a fallen world. We can glean from the actions and words of Jesus and learn from the mistakes and revelations of the disciples.

> *Then the apostles gathered to Jesus and told Him all things, both what they had done and what they had taught. And He said to them, "Come aside by yourselves to a deserted place and rest a while." For there were many coming and going, and they did not even have time to eat. So they departed to a deserted place in the boat by themselves.*

We are about to read one of the most famous miracles in the Bible, the multiplication of the loaves and fishes. It is interesting to point out that before the disciples were commissioned to perform a miracle, Jesus commanded them to begin in a posture of rest and positioned in the presence of God. Jesus had just received the news of John the Baptist being beheaded, and it is wise to heed the action of Jesus—He rested. It is easy for us to go from one errand to another and meet the needs of every issue or problem in our day and completely forget the power of rest and the presence of God. The simple but profound truth is that you cannot walk in authority unless you are under authority. Jesus prayed short and simple prayers. Our Lord was never in a hurry and was completely reliant on the presence and voice of the Father (John 15). If Jesus needed the power of the Holy Spirit, rest, and the voice of the Father, how much more you and I?

*But the multitude saw them departing, and many knew
Him and ran there on foot from all the cities. They arrived
before them and came together to Him. And Jesus, when
He came out, saw a great multitude and was moved with
compassion for them, because they were like sheep not having
a shepherd. So He began to teach them many things.*

The second thing we notice from the actions of Jesus in this chapter is that He had *compassion* on the multitude. This speaks volumes to me. We can easily fall into the trap that because I have authority, all *my* needs can be met, but we turn off our focus on serving others. Jesus came to serve and not be served (Mark 10:45). A person who is secure in their identity and who is spiritually mature will have a natural focus on other people. If you are confident that God has taken care of your needs, then you have the freedom to focus on the needs of those around you.

We see examples of misguided authority all the time. It is either you are so self-focused and hoard the power of God so that no one is blessed by you, or you are unaware of your authority and become absorbed in other people's needs first. Both are unhealthy. We cannot give away what we don't have or are ignorant about. There is value in taking care of your needs and being sure of God's love for you before you minister to others. It is much like a marriage relationship where both husband and wife must have their needs met first before they can give to the other. You can either be a conduit or vacuum depending on your perspective and understanding.

*When the day was now far spent, His disciples came to Him and said, "This is a deserted place, and already the hour is late. Send them away, that they may go into the surrounding country and villages and buy themselves bread; for they have nothing to eat."*
*But He answered and said to them, "You give them something to eat."*

Jesus and the disciples were aware of the need. The multitude was so engaged in the revelation of what Jesus was teaching that they didn't even eat. So much so that Jesus knew if they were sent away and didn't have something to eat, they would faint. I love the innocence of the disciples and how they first reacted to the natural. The disciples began looking to human effort to find a solution in feeding the thousands in attendance. But Jesus rained in on their parade when He said, *"You give them something to eat."*

There is a powerful truth that God, even in His sovereignty, will not interfere with what He has given us authority to accomplish. Take for example my son. As a five-year-old he has homework that I could accomplish in seconds what would take him over half an hour to finish. It would be easy for me to step in and do it all for him, yet I would be robbing him of confidence, growth, and satisfaction of using his own gifts and intelligence.

Can God end world hunger? Yes. Can God remove all the evil in the world in a split second? Yes. But He continues to give us free will in this world and uses normal, everyday people like you and me to accomplish His will. I cannot stand the pointed fingers at God when tragedy arises. People automatically turn all the blame on God when evil has a victory. When people were murdered and kidnapped in Mexico, people point the finger at

God because "He allowed it to happen." We forget the whole time that though it "was allowed," God *also* commissioned believers with the power that conquered the grave to *go over to* Mexico and put an end to the violence themselves. If God's power dwells in you and me, then we have just as much responsibility to handle the issues of the world. Praise God though because we not only have a responsibility to change the world, but we have also been given the answer! We are not without hope, and we have not been released into this world without being equipped and clothed in power from on high!

However, the disciples, like you and me, when we are outside our comfort zone, immediately put up excuses:

*And they said to Him, "Shall we go and buy two hundred denarii worth of bread and give them something to eat?"*

*Jesus dismantled their excuses with a challenge that is for all of us as well:*

*But He said to them, "How many loaves do you have? Go and see. (emphasis mine)*

The disciples had been in the presence of God and came from a place of rest. They had been given authority and a command by God to meet the people's need. When the disciples offered up an excuse that they didn't have the resources to meet the need, Jesus simply redirected their focus to what they *did have*. I love this powerful truth. We need to stop looking at what we don't have or what we feel God is "not doing/answering" and start releasing what we do have and what He has promised. If God said it, you should have all confidence that He will supply your every need to not only survive it but also to see incredible victory!

The next important example we must focus on is *how* Jesus released the miracle:

*Then He commanded them to make them all sit down in groups on the green grass. So they sat down in ranks, in hundreds and in fifties. And when He had taken the five loaves and the two fish, He **looked up to heaven, blessed** and broke the loaves, and gave them to His disciples to set before them; and the two fish He divided among them all. So they all ate and were filled. And they took up twelve baskets full of fragments and of the fish. Now those who had eaten the loaves were about five thousand men.*

Jesus set the people up to receive a miracle. I pray that at your church, ministry, or home you position yourself and those close to you for a miracle. As the multitude was seated, Jesus *looked up to heaven.* While the disciples looked to the world and human effort to meet the need, Jesus looked up to heaven. We must have the perspective of heaven and again see everything in this life through the lens of the realities of heaven. Jesus looked to the answer, not the lack. He focused on the promise, not the problem.

After Jesus looked up to heaven, He blessed and broke the bread. Jesus gave thanks for the miracle *before* He even passed out the first sandwich. I am fully confident Jesus had no hesitation or reservation that God would be faithful and would multiply that food. It is critically important that as believers we walk around in life with the expectation that God will be faithful to carry out what He has promised. When we are faced with a problem, we must train ourselves to expect good things and that we will quickly be on the other side of testimony because of the power of God.

## *Guarding Your Heart*

The last thing I want to mention is what happened *after* the miracle. It is so easy to see God's power move and then put our faith in autopilot. There is work to be done after the miracle, and it is really the *only* work that we as believers must do. We must guard our hearts. Again the Hebrew word for *heart* literally means "seat of thoughts." Take a look at what happened with the disciples after the miracle of the multiplication:

*Immediately He made His disciples get into the boat and go before Him to the other side, to Bethsaida, while He sent the multitude away. And when He had sent them away, **He departed** to the mountain to pray. Now when evening came, the boat was in the middle of the sea; and He was alone on the land. Then **He saw** them straining at rowing, for the wind was against them. Now about the fourth watch of the night **He came to them,** walking on the sea, and would have passed them by. And when they saw Him walking on the sea, they supposed it was a ghost, and cried out; for they all saw Him and were troubled. But immediately He talked with them and said to them, **"Be of good cheer! It is I; do not be afraid."** Then He went up into the boat to them, and the wind ceased. And they were greatly amazed in themselves beyond*

> *measure, and marveled.* **For they had not understood** *about the loaves, because their heart was hardened. (emphasis mine)*

There is so much packed into this one passage of scripture but such amazing revelation. The disciples were immediately given a new command to go across the sea, then Jesus *departed*. The disciples were about to face a life-threatening storm and Jesus *left them?* First off, though Jesus departed, He wasn't very far. What is amazing though is that from what I know, the Sea of Galilee is seven miles wide and thirteen miles long, which means if the disciples were in *the middle* of the sea and Jesus was on the land, He could still see them, even in the poor visibility of the storm (verse 48). This gives me hope that God is always watching and is always near in our times of trouble. Though we may feel that He is a million miles away, He is closer than we think.

Jesus climbed in the boat and the storm instantly died down. They were reminded again of the power of God, and Jesus gave them the encouragement to "not be afraid." The disciples still didn't understand the power that was available for them and the authority they had because of their hard hearts. When I think of a hard heart, I automatically go back to the days when the Israelites were captives in Egypt and Moses was being hindered from releasing the Israelites because of Pharaoh's hard heart. To have a hard heart is more than just a rebellion and stubbornness against God; it is being unaware, distracted, and focused on the wrong things. The disciples did nothing wrong in that boat in the middle of the storm. They reacted probably in the same way that most anyone would, yet they did not experience the miracle they needed because of a wrong focus.

## *Don't Miss Out*

I was blessed the other day when I was spending some time with my son. He was having an issue finding a very small toy that I had just bought him. As we looked under sofas and in the car, my son paused and said in his five-year-old voice, "Daddy, it's okay. I will pray for Jesus to find it." He said a very quick prayer, and literally two seconds later, we found the toy. This is a very small example of walking in the closeness of God and understanding identity. My son attends our children's ministry here at my church where three- to ten-year-olds are growing in the power of God and are doing so with childlike faith and without all the limits we adults place on God.

You have probably said it or heard a million times, "I wish I knew then what I know now." I am confident that my son will reach levels in his life and ministry because he is springboarding off the revelation I have received over the years. He doesn't have to make the same mistakes I did. He can go so much farther than I have and so much quicker. Let this be an encouragement to you that now is the time to learn all that the Lord has given you and to begin taking risks by exercising your authority in all different aspects of life. God has given us all we need in life for victory and joy. We have incredible authority in this life. Let us keep our focus on what we do have rather than what is around us.

# Chapter 5

## *Taking the Fair Out of Warfare*

I WAS BLESSED AS A child to have grown up in a neighborhood where almost every home had a kid around my age. This was before the days of Nintendo Wii and Xbox. The days where we didn't pretend to play baseball with a wireless remote control, we actually went *outside* and played the real thing! Every summer was different depending on what the latest trend was. One summer a kid in the neighborhood got a pair of Rollerblades. Soon it was as if we had started our own street hockey team as everyone convinced their parents to get them a pair. On one occasion a dad had gotten his child a rollaway basketball hoop and set it out on the curb; another summer it was our bikes with cardboard racing numbers on the front and a deck of cards in the spokes of our wheels.

Those days were fun, but I will never forget a day when we were all outside playing with a Frisbee. One kid had thrown it too far and it went over a short fence of a neighbor's front yard. My friend quickly hopped over the fence to retrieve the Frisbee but was viciously mauled by the neighbor's two large dogs. From that time up until this day, I still have a slight fear of larger dogs.

I had my own brutal encounter with a large neighborhood dog, though it was more on my part than it was the dog's. One day as I was riding my bike on an early Saturday morning, I noticed a golden retriever sitting in the front yard of a house about four away from mine. The dog was watching my every move, and I rode in confidence thinking that though there was not a fence to keep the dog contained, surely he was tied to a chain or rope. When the dog got up and started bolting after me, I quickly realized the dog was not tied down. This golden retriever was out to retrieve me! I quickly flipped my bike around and pedaled as hard as my skinny little seven-year-old legs could go. The scene could have been in the movies. As I looked back, the dog was inching closer and closer, dripping fangs moments away from my back tire, life flashing before my eyes, then as the dog was about to succeed in the hunt . . . *bam!* I had crashed head-on into a parked van. The dog even stopped in his tracks and gave me a look that said, "Wow, that was stupid." With adrenaline still coursing through my veins, it was as if the impact had no effect. I got up, grabbed my bike, and proceeded to my garage and into the safety of my home.

Do you know the reason I got hurt that day? I was looking at the dog and not looking ahead. I was focused on my problem and not my destination. I share this example to demonstrate the pattern that we fall into. In our battle with the enemy, we are continuing to fix our focus and attention on what he is doing rather than on where the Lord is taking us. We are not seeing the devil as a defeated foe. Rather, we view him as someone with power, if not one with more power than we have. This is completely wrong.

From the very beginning, even with Adam and Eve, the devil's strategy has been the same, deception and distraction:

*He was a murderer from the beginning, not holding to the truth,
for there is no truth in him. When he lies, he speaks his native
language, for he is a liar and the father of lies. (John 8:44)*

The devil doesn't have to "attack you" or "oppress you" in order to have victory in your life. He simply needs you to buy into what he is selling; we end up doing the rest. To clarify this more, think about the last "failure" you had or sin that you fell into. I can guarantee that it all began with a single thought. Let's say that you are struggling right now with an alcohol addiction. The problem didn't come when you got home from work and drowned your pain and sorrows with the bottle; the problem came earlier in the day when the enemy whispered a lie into your ear. He said, "Wow, it's been a long week. There's so much pressure on you right now, your wife is giving you the hardest time at home, and at this age you should be so much further up the ladder." We buy into the deception and become distracted from the truth found in God's presence and Word. By day's end we have convinced ourselves that it will not be a big deal, that it's only a little sin, and that we deserve it after all that we have just gone through. We find ourselves in bondage and never realize that if we stopped the enemy at his *first word*, we would be walking in complete freedom.

I want to take you through a small time line of the rise and fall of Satan and bring to light the incredible power and authority that Jesus has given and expose how defeated and harmless the devil really is. In my opinion, if there is no darkness or devil in heaven, there should be no darkness or devil in the lives of believers who are citizens of heaven (Philippians 3:20).

# *In the Beginning, God Gave Authority and Power to Man*

*Then God said, "Let Us make man in Our image, according to Our likeness; let them have dominion. —Genesis 1:26*

*God blessed them and said to them, "Be fruitful and increase in number; fill the earth and **subdue** it. **Rule** over."—Genesis 1:28*

In the beginning God created the heavens and the earth and then filled it with all things that "were good." He created man to have relationship with and blessed them with power and authority. There was no sin, no sorrow, no sickness, and no separation. Adam and Eve had wonderful communion with God, lived with no shame, and were blessed in all that they did. You could say they were living a true "heaven on earth" experience.

God's original plan was that man would be in charge of earth and grow in relationship with Him, to enjoy His presence, and to live a life to its fullest. However, God was not in the business of making robots or forcing people into love; therefore, He gave man free will. We were to bear the choice of following God or following sin.

## *Satan Fell from Heaven*

*How you have fallen from heaven, morning star, son of the dawn! You have been cast down to the earth, you who once laid low the nations! You said in your heart, "I will ascend to the heavens; I will raise my throne above the stars of God; I will sit enthroned on the mount of assembly, on the utmost heights of Mount Zaphon. I will ascend above the tops of the clouds; I will make myself like the Most High." But you are brought down to the realm of the dead, to the depths of the pit."—Isaiah 14:12–15*

Though man and woman lived in a perfect world with a perfect god, there was still a sinful being roaming the earth. We all know of the account found in Genesis 3 where Adam and Eve ate the fruit and became deceived by the enemy.

*Then the LORD God said to the woman, "What is this you have done?" The woman said, "The serpent deceived me, and I ate." (Genesis 3:13)*

Some people actually take time to debate whether it was the woman's fault or the man's fault for falling into sin and cursing mankind. The simple truth is that though Eve partook of the fruit, Adam was standing right beside her! In fact Genesis 3:6 says, "She also gave some to her husband, who was with her, and he ate it." To all the men reading this, I don't know about you, but if a snake is talking to my lady, some sleeves will be rolled up, if you know what I mean. Both man and woman were deceived, and it says "their eyes were opened" (Genesis 3:7).

God had given man authority over the earth, but man had handed over authority to the devil when they agreed with his deception and proceeded to sin. We can clearly see the short reign of Satan, who is called the "prince of the world" (John 12:31) throughout the Old Testament. Take into consideration this verse:

*And the devil said to Him, "All this **authority** I will give You,*
*and their glory; for this has been delivered to me, and I give it*
*to whomever I wish. (Luke 4:6; notice the devil had authority)*

When the devil came to tempt Jesus and had *authority* available
to give away, Satan received that authority from man. The devil,
throughout the old covenant, continued to prowl around through
the earth and oppress the people of God:

*And the LORD said to Satan, "From where do you come?"*
*So Satan answered the LORD and said, "From going to and fro*
*on the earth, and from walking back and forth on it." (Job 1:7)*

### Jesus Came to Restore the Authority That Was Lost

I remember when my son was around three years, there was
a week when he would wake up screaming as if something were
after him. At two o'clock in the morning for a couple of days,
an episode of fear would come over him. We had a baby gate in
the hallway by his room to prevent him from wandering in the
kitchen or a place of harm in the middle of the night. When
these terrors came upon him, I would find my son trying to climb
over the gate and looking behind him as if something were after
him. I would go in the room and find nothing wrong, but for a
few nights my son would end up in our bed in the early morning
hours.

I could not figure out the problem, and though we had prayed
over my son and stood upon the truth that our house was blessed
and anointed and the enemy had no authority or welcome, my

son was still in fear. The last night that this episode happened, I was able to finally figure out the cause. Sure enough at two in the morning, the screaming began. I ran to his room faster this time and lifted the baby gate, freeing him to quickly run into our room. This episode was different from the rest as I heard an intense growling inside his room. I was excited to go do some battle for my son. To my surprise I had found the "demon" to only be his Disney *Cars* alarm clock. It had somehow set for two in the morning, and the alarm was the sound of an engine revving up. My poor little son was being startled awake from something he had complete control over.

The clock was a Christmas gift from his great-grandmother, so we couldn't just put it away or give it away. So to prove to my son that this clock would no longer terrify him, I removed the batteries. *One day* we will completely get rid of the clock, but for the time being I rendered it harmless and *powerless*. The same is exactly true for you and me. Though God has not completely removed Satan from the earth, He has taken away his power completely. Jesus came to restore the authority that was lost and put man back into his rightly place with power, authority, and dominion.

*Jesus spoke these words, lifted up His eyes to heaven, and said: "Father, the hour has come. Glorify Your Son, that Your Son also may glorify You, as You have given Him **authority over all flesh**, that He should **give** eternal life to as many as You have given Him. And this is eternal life, that they may know You, the only true God, and Jesus Christ whom You have sent. (John 17:1–3)*

Jesus destroyed all of Satan's power and authority on the cross. Jesus spoke powerful words when He said, "It is finished" (John 19:30). The old covenant was gone and the new covenant had begun. Satan's authority was taken and man was freed of the devil's bondage once and for all.

*The reason the Son of God appeared was to*
*destroy the devil's work. (1 John 3:8)*

*Since the children have flesh and blood, he too shared in their*
*humanity so that by his death he might break the power of him*
*who holds the power of death—that is, the devil. (Hebrews 2:14)*

## Keys to the Kingdom

With freedom comes responsibility. The Bible says in Luke 12:32, "Do not fear, little flock, for it is your Father's good pleasure to give you the kingdom." Though the Lord has given us the keys to His kingdom and blessed us with freedom, it does not mean that we go idle and remain fruitless.

I love the statement and phrase "I don't have time to be messing with the devil." Take a glance at some of the commands Jesus gave to us:

*Then He called His twelve disciples together and gave them power*
*and **authority** over **all** demons, and to cure diseases. (Luke 9:1)*

> *Behold, I give you the **authority** to trample on serpents*
> *and scorpions, and over **all** the power of the enemy, and*
> *nothing shall by any means hurt you. (Luke 10:19)*

> *And Jesus came and spoke to them, saying, "**All authority** has*
> *been given to Me in heaven and on earth. Go therefore and make*
> *disciples of all the nations, baptizing them in the name of the*
> *Father and of the Son and of the Holy Spirit." (Matthew 28:18)*

About a year ago my wife and I purchased a Jeep Commander, which is a midsize sports utility vehicle. We were driving a Ford Focus, which is a compact car. As my son continued to grow, it became evident that we needed a bigger car when he began using my shoulders as a foot rest from his car seat behind me. Many of the newer Chrysler vehicles have a larger two-in-one remote and key. Rather than insert a traditional metal key in the ignition, the entire remote/key combination is placed in the ignition. It is fun to watch people at the car wash or the mechanics when I take it in for maintenance attempt to figure the thing out. One thing is certain; if you don't know how to use the key, you won't go anywhere.

Anyone can read the owner's manual to a car, but there is a big difference between just knowing about the car and actually driving the car. There is a combination of knowing and doing. The same is true in the spiritual sense. We may read and reread the manual (Bible) but never apply or do what it says we can do. There are many factors that keep Christians paralyzed in their faith, including fear, insecurity, ignorance, and sin; however, the main hindrance is continuing to agree with the devil's lie. Though the devil has ultimately been defeated, he still has a mouth. It is similar to a death row inmate. They are behind bars and sentenced to death. They are no longer a danger to society, yet they still have freedom of speech. This truth is liberating in knowing that the battle we face with Satan is no longer in the physical, but spiritual. This means that our entire battle with Satan is fought in our minds. If you can discipline yourself with a renewed mind (Romans 12:2) you have complete victory in your life.

*"For our struggle is not against flesh and blood, but against the rulers, against the authorities, against the powers of this dark world and against the spiritual forces of evil in the heavenly realms."—Ephesians 6:12*

We cannot walk around defeated and powerless when we know that we have victory and authority over the devil!

*"I have given you authority to trample on snakes and scorpions and to overcome all the power of the enemy; **nothing will harm you.**"—Luke 10:19 (Emphasis mine)*

If you want real entertainment in life, you need not see a movie. Simply go to a church that feels they have to battle Satan because he has power. When people are prayed for to be delivered of a demon, it is quite a show. There is screaming, rocking, yelling, threatening, and so forth. The Bible is very clear with Jesus's examples that we don't have to do these unnecessary tactics. Jesus time and time again cast demons out with a single word (Matthew 8:16), Jesus told demons to be quiet (Mark 1:25), and He never had to argue, but simply *stood* on His authority and what God had promised. The Bible tells us to do the same. Take a look at the famous account of spiritual warfare found in Ephesians 6:

## Real Warfare

*Therefore take up the whole armor of God, that you may be able to withstand in the evil day, and having done all, to stand. Stand therefore, having girded your waist with truth, having put on the breastplate of righteousness, and having shod your feet with the preparation of the gospel of peace; above all, taking the shield of faith with which you will be able to quench all the fiery darts of the wicked one. And take the helmet of salvation, and the sword of the Spirit, which is the word of God; praying always with all prayer and supplication in the Spirit.*

This passage has been preached so many times and for so many centuries. I am certain there are hundreds of pastors and teachers far more qualified to teach and expand on this subject, but allow me to shed some light on a few things:

## 1. Take a stand.

Notice about four times in Ephesians chapter 6, it states that we must "stand." When I take a stand, it means that I am convinced and have made up my mind. We do not have to go to battle with the enemy. Noticed the passage says nothing about *fighting* the devil, just standing against him; again he is nothing but a mouth.

## 2. Stand in truth.

The Bible says in John 8:32 that "the truth will make you free." Some versions say "set you free," but freedom does not come *to you*; it is released *through you*. We have freedom already because Jesus lives in us and died for us. When we come into agreement that the devil has already been defeated and we have complete victory, it makes a "battle" so much easier. If you are not convinced that the battle has already been won, you will continue to go in circles fighting an imaginary war.

## 3. Stand in identity.

The breastplate covers and protects all the vital organs, especially the heart. Satan is after your identity and will continue to attempt to deceive you. The devil will try and try to convince you that you are worthless, sinful, and weak. The truth is that we are in right standing with God because of the sacrifice of Jesus and are dead to sin and alive in Him (Romans 6:11). We have incredible identity in Christ. We cannot afford to keep living with the thought of what we once were and forget about what we have been called since the beginning of time. Jesus died for all our sins, past, present, and future. We must live with the lens of heaven and see ourselves as God sees us (Romans 8).

## 4. Stand in peace.

Ephesians says to "shod your feet with . . . the Gospel of peace." Many people enjoy testimony and stories of spiritual warfare. You have everyone's attention when you get ready to tell a scary story about an encounter with a demon and how ugly and powerful they looked. Spiritual warfare has brought fear mainly because of Hollywood and wrong thinking. Peace is one of the most powerful weapons and tools the believer has been given by Jesus. The enemy can handle your loud and dramatic prayers against him, he can even do battle with you in the scriptures and try to twist them, but He cannot handle it when you are at rest, trust, and peace. You know you have peace when you are fully aware of what God has done for you and how powerless the devil really is. Our worship pastor Greeyvin Camacho once said, "I have come to the realization that in this life I can either worry or worship."

## 5. Take the helmet of salvation.

It is interesting that the helmet of salvation is something that protects and covers you mind. As I said before, salvation is more than just a free ticket to heaven. Jesus came that we might have all freedom, power, and authority. You will have complete control and have the battle completely won if you can stop the enemy at the first thought. We must remind ourselves of the power of what God has done for us and not let the enemy convince us otherwise.

There is a need to have our minds "protected" by the truth of the Gospel. We bear the responsibility of applying what we have been given into our world and denying any lie that may come against it. The responsibility that we have in God should not be dreaded as He has taken care of everything we will ever face in life through His blood. The enemy will be rendered completely harmless and void in your life if you simply guard your thoughts and focus on God's Word.

I am not a big breakfast or lunch kind of guy. Typically I like something that is fast and easy when it comes to the first meals of the day. Dinnertime, however, is something I look forward to. I am the cook in the family, and throughout my day I will go over in my mind the things I need for a wonderful meal with my family. The problem comes when my family switches the meal plan last minute. If I have a homemade pizza in my mind, I don't want burgers. All day long I have fantasized about pizza; a burger has no lure to me whatsoever. The same is true for our daily fight against the devil's lies. If you are not thinking about a certain thing, the devil cannot tempt or lure you with it. If you guard your thoughts, you have rendered him powerless.

## 6. Our weapons.

I have heard it said by many preachers that in all the armor of God, there is nothing covering the believer's back because we were never designed to flee from battle. At the same time, however, we are not to go out looking for the devil or engage with him in any way; this is simply stupid. There is no reason to have any contact or conversation with the devil, period. We are only to "do battle" when he is on the attack. Notice that the only weapon we have to defeat the demons or the devil is the sword (Word of God) and praying in the Spirit. We see this modeled in the temptation and life of Jesus.

## *How Jesus Handled the Devil*

The devil's tricks and tools have not changed throughout time. His main weapons are pride and false identity. Satan's desire is to turn your focus from God to yourself. By turning you inward, he will succeed in making you unaware of God's presence—ultimately, His help and power. The devil does this by convincing you that you are something you are not (identity) and attempts to get you to get something you already have, by way of sin (pride).

In Genesis chapter 3 we see the devil tempting Adam and Eve in the Garden of Eden with the same things that he tempted Jesus with in the wilderness. Adam and Eve failed and fell into temptation whereas Jesus shows us how to properly eliminate satanic influence. Remember, we can do the things Jesus did as a man but cannot do the things He did as God (John 14:12). If we see Jesus model something that we as humans can do, we must be active at pursuing and demonstrating those things. Let's take a quick look at the account of Jesus's temptation and see His responses:

*Then Jesus was led up by the Spirit into the wilderness to be tempted by the devil. And when He had fasted forty days and forty nights, afterward He was hungry. (Matthew 4:1–2)*

The enemy is an opportunist and will attempt to hit you while you're down. Jesus was fasting for forty days with no food and was in a wilderness environment. I get irritable and grumpy if I simply miss a meal. I cannot imagine forty days without food and in an uncomfortable and dangerous environment.

The devil came to Jesus while He was hungry and outside His normal surroundings. Jesus was completely unaffected by His circumstances. Jesus said in John 16:33, "In the world you will have tribulation; but be of good cheer, I have overcome the world." Your circumstances seem obsolete in comparison to who you are and what you have been given. The key to being uninfluenced by your circumstances is to have a clear focus on God.

*Now when the tempter came to Him, he said, "If You are the Son of God, command that these stones become bread." (Matthew 4:3)*

After the enemy attempted to bring Jesus down by attacking any possible weaknesses, he went after Jesus's identity. The enemy said, "*If* you are the Son of God." The tempter did not articulate that Jesus *was* the Son of God, he said, "*If.*" If the enemy can take your eyes off who you are, he can convince you of what you are not. Jesus was confident in His identity. Jesus had just been baptized before being led by the Spirit into the wilderness. One of the most critical things that took place in the baptism of Jesus was the words spoken by God the Father, "This is My beloved Son, in whom I am well pleased" (Matthew 3:17). Before Jesus was a miracle worker, preacher, or healer, He was a son. Jesus knew His identity and He knew it from His Daddy. No demon, devil, or punk would convince Him otherwise, and you and I need to do the same. Father God has spoken tremendous truth over our lives, and we cannot let the darkness of this world lead us to believe a lie about our identity in Him.

What I love so much about this story is that when Jesus was faithful and took a stance, unmoved by the devil, it says that angels came and ministered to Him (Matthew 4:11). When

Adam and Eve failed the test, the Bible says they "hid from the Lord" (Genesis 3:8). Having the right perspective of who we are in Christ draws us closer in intimacy with the Father. A recognition of our failures and sins will draw us away from His love.

*But He answered and said, "It is written." (Matthew 4:4)*

Satan is aware of the scriptures. The Bible says in Luke 2:19, "You believe that there is one God. You do well. Even the demons believe—and tremble! The fact that Satan knows the scriptures is revealed in verses 5 and 6, where Satan uses the Word to tempt Jesus to throw Himself down from the pinnacle of the temple. The simple fact that Satan knows the Word of God should give you the motivation to know it for yourself. In the midst of the attack, Jesus simply fought back with the *truth* of the Word and said, "It is written."

If we are not Bible literate, how do we expect to stand up the twisting of scripture that the devil throws our way? How many times have we found ourselves justifying sin with scripture? We must know the Bible fully and let it be the basis in which all our actions and decisions are made.

*Then Jesus said to him, "Away with you, Satan! For it is written, 'You shall worship the LORD your God, and Him only you shall serve.'" (Matthew 4:10)*

The last pathetic attempt of the enemy was to try to convince Jesus to worship him if he gave Jesus all kingdoms of the world (Matthew 4:8–9). Again, the devil was trying to tempt with something he knew we already have. Jesus already had power over the devil and would soon take back the keys of the kingdom of God and give them to us. Jesus does not only own all the kingdoms of the world, but He also owns the kingdom of God and the universe. We cannot fall victim to the lie that we need something we already have. In no way can sin fulfill us like the truth of what God has given, and we cannot use shortcuts to receive peace and satisfaction; they are only found in Christ and Christ alone.

# Chapter 6

## *Runaway Bride*

As the clouds rolled in, so did our fears. The forecast had been calling for rain all weekend long, yet our God was calling us to fulfill the mission He had given to us. So with an unwavering confidence, the band began setting up the stage. Instruments were being set in place, plugged in, and then checked for proper sound levels.

Laughter filled the air as the nearly hundred volunteers went about setting all kinds of things in place. The games were set up and tested out. A team had pulled out the barbecue grills and began organizing a thousand dollars' worth of hamburgers and hotdogs. Twelve hundred plastic chairs borrowed from surrounding churches were neatly set in place on our dirt lot. A group of about a dozen ladies enjoyed the overwhelming task of separating and organizing truckloads of clothing and giveaways. Kids from off the street began showing up to see all the excitement that they would be able to partake of in just a few hours.

Every year our church sends a talented team of Spanish- and English-speaking staff and volunteers to the busy and dusty streets of Tijuana, Mexico. Any headline about crime or any rumor about homicide would be enough to keep most Christians north of the border. We decided, not only will we go to one of the most dangerous places in the world, but we will also do it on the darkest day of the year—Halloween. Why not? We are called to be lights, and light always wins against the darkness.

The year before, we saw dozens commit their lives to Jesus. We saw little kids with dirty feet receive a new pair of shoes. We saw illnesses healed on the spot. Worship music was played with a canvas of beautiful graffiti behind us, a busy intersection in front of us, and dozens of poorly constructed homes all around us. Over a thousand people showed up to the carnival this year, and this year we expected God to double the attendance, double the salvations, and double the miracles. But as the drizzle began to turn our dirt lot into a mud floor, worries began to rise. The drizzle turned to rain and the rain turned into a downpour. All volunteers and work came to a complete halt as the band scrambled to cover anything plugged into an extension cord with plastic. Everyone scurried under whatever tent or open tailgate they could find to stay dry.

Even as a pastor, I was among the conversations that began doubting. People were saying things like "At least we brought all this stuff to give away" and "Well, you know, you can't control the rain." It looked as if our event would be called off because of something as puny as bad weather.

After a half an hour of hiding out, our team leader, Dayan Garcia, called everyone in for a meeting. In the back of my mind I was thinking he would be giving us new directions on how to shut down the event or possibly move all the tents together to organize and give away all the clothes, food, and gifts. What I heard next will remain with me for a lifetime.

Dayan stood up on a plastic chair with all the volunteers surrounding him and said, "I'm not giving up. This rain is nothing compared to how big my God is."

I was stunned at my lack of faith and tremendously inspired by Dayan's leadership. We indeed serve a big God, and it was His idea to do this outreach, so He would be faithful to give us all we needed not only to survive the event but also to see it be a success. We all lifted our hands to the heavens and rebuked the rain. Within a half hour, the rain had disappeared and the sun came out not only to pay us a visit, but also to dry up the sky and land. The work resumed, and we went on to see God do above and beyond what we could have expected.

No one would have thought negatively if Dayan decided to cancel the event. Many would have viewed it simply as God's will and that it's the thought that counts. Dayan took matters into his own hands by simply standing on the truth of what the Word says. God is bigger than anything we will ever face, and we have the authority to change our circumstances. We were blessed with the honor of experiencing this reality firsthand that day in Tijuana.

That day holds such a special place in my heart as I witnessed so many of the realities of heaven played out in my world. Everyone worked in unison, and joy abounded as we worked, yet laughed and enjoyed fellowship. We worshiped God together in the open air, and the truth of the Gospel was preached. Hundreds came to know the Lord and enter His kingdom that day. We prayed for people and saw mighty miracles. Thousands of people were fed and clothed. Even the weather bowed down to the name of Jesus that day. Yet the most amazing thing of that day was the collective expectation that filled the air. No one was begging God to do something that day; we operated with thankful hearts of what God had already accomplished for us on the cross and stepped into the role of our authority.

## The Normal Christian Life

It is my personal opinion that a revival began in the first church that was only meant to continue to build throughout time. What took place that night at our church was amazing, yet in comparison to what the Bible speaks about the power of God, it was just a normal day, something to be expected every day for anyone who believes. Unfortunately we do not see a strong manifestation of the raw power of God in most churches today. Though God is doing mighty work, people are getting saved, set free, and discipled; we should be looking at the church in the days of Peter and Paul as a reference point and building upon it generation after generation.

Though I firmly believe that the power of God should be demonstrated in the church, I do understand that there have been some abuses in the past. Some have used a gift given by God and used it for personal gain either for fame or finances. Many who walked in the supernatural and the power of God did not remain pure and faithful throughout their entire lives. Yet we cannot ignore God's original intention for the church based upon a few poor stewards.

We have all types of extremes in the church world. There are the "turn or burn" preachers, the "name it and claim it," and the "frozen chosen." Regardless of denomination or style, we should all aim for the heartbeat of heaven and the model set forth by Jesus in the first-century church. We should dare to believe that people who go to church today should be the happiest, most well-off, most loving, and most talented people in the world. If we believe, truly, what the Bible says about God's power, what Jesus died for and our identity, we should bear no shame to desire to be on top of every spectrum of life here on earth.

In the New Testament church we read of healings, miracles, signs, and wonders. People gave to those who had in need and shared all things in common. There was fellowship, Bible study, and extreme devotion (Acts 2:42–47). We must expect more from the church than just four pretty songs of worship, some announcements, and a thirty-minute sermon. The church, in the words of Pastor Bill Hybels, is the "hope of the world." As believers we should be equipped to handle all life's problems through the blood of Jesus and the power of God. Everything, from our sicknesses, poverty, relational issues, and emotional wounds. We should not just applaud the heroes of the faith, the evangelists, and the mega church pastors. Each one of us in the body of Christ should be walking in destiny and releasing the power of God. A beautiful example of a true picture of church is found in a story of two apostles going to church:

*Now Peter and John went up together to the temple at the hour of prayer, the ninth hour. And a certain man lame from his mother's womb was carried, whom they laid daily at the gate of the temple which is called Beautiful, to ask alms from those who entered the temple; who, seeing Peter and John about to go into the temple, asked for alms. And fixing his eyes on him, with John, Peter said, "Look at us." So he gave them his attention, expecting to receive something from them.*

The first thing that stuck me when reading this passage of scripture was the fact that Peter and John were simply on their way to "church" yet had their eyes open and their hearts willing wherever they went. They did not limit what could be done through the power of God to the inside of the temple; they also had their eyes open to what was going on *outside*. We have to consciously purpose to not limit our availability to spreading the gospel to church services and outreach events. Whether we are in a Starbucks, grocery store, park, or school, we must be aware that we carry the presence of God and have the command to release heaven on earth.

If you have ever been on a missions trip or served at an outreach, then you know the "high" you get after ministering God's love to strangers and those with needs. It is a wonderful feeling to be used by God and to see firsthand the fruit of applying your faith to your feet. The truth is that we do not have to wait for a church event or outreach to be used by God. You have an opportunity every second of the day, whether it be with your family, boss, coworker, or complete stranger. We must live with an awareness that we are instruments of God and can lead a person at any time into a miracle and the life-transforming power of salvation. Jesus spoke of the importance of reaching all people with the power of God in Luke 4:17–19:

*And He was handed the book of the prophet Isaiah. And when He had opened the book, He found the place where it was written:*
*"The Spirit of the LORD is upon Me,*
*Because He has anointed Me*
*To preach the gospel to the poor;*
*He has sent Me to heal the brokenhearted,*
*To proclaim liberty to the captives*
*And recovery of sight to the blind,*
*To set at liberty those who are oppressed;*
*To proclaim the acceptable year of the LORD."*

Jesus's passion was simple, He wanted to only do what He saw the Father doing and was willing to die for it (John 5:19). We know that it is the Father's good pleasure to give us the kingdom of God (Luke 12:32), so we can expect that His will is to see His children live on earth with the reality of the kingdom of heaven (no sorrow, sin, sickness, or suffering). And if Jesus only did what He saw the Father doing, then we can interpret Jesus's earthly ministry to be the will of the Father. A majority of Jesus's ministry on earth was healing the sick, casting out demons, and preaching the Gospel. The Lord also promised us that we could do what He did and "even greater works" (John 14:12). This thought gives me a challenge to keep my spiritual eyes open to the needs around me at all times and in all situations. I must look for opportunities to spread God's love and power to my life and the lives around me. Let us continue in Acts chapter 3:

> *Then Peter said, "Silver and gold I do not have, but what I do have I give you: In the name of Jesus Christ of Nazareth, rise up and walk." And he took him by the right hand and lifted him up, and immediately his feet and ankle bones received strength.*

Peter exercised an important character trait that we must all possess, the power of focusing on what you do have rather than what you don't. Peter may have not been able to minister to this man's material need of having no money, but Peter was carrying the power of God and was able to meet a physical need of healing the man's paralysis.

It is easy to remain complacent in our faith when we focus on what we lack. A powerful truth I discovered early on in life is that if I want something bad enough, I will get it! I will find a way through adversity, oppression, and obstacle to gain what I desire. We see this all the time in all areas of life. I remember when I was first getting to know my wife, before we began dating. We would stay at a local Starbucks for four to five hours at a time talking about *nothing*! We would then go home and talk on the phone until two in the morning even though we both had full-time jobs. If you truly want something bad enough, you'll get it. The same is true in the spiritual world. If you desire a breakthrough or to be used in a greater measure, you can have it, as long as you truly desire it. But focusing on your limitations and lack will only paralyze you in your faith and success. We have to look to God's finished work, not the works of man.

When I was in high school, there was a kid named Cisco, who walked around campus with two things: a big water bottle and a big Bible. He was a humble person with wisdom beyond his years. Everyone knew him not as a person who tried too hard to be Christian but leaked out the love of God. I will never forget one lunch period when I looked over to the corner of the quad to see a large gathering of people in excitement. Normally this means a schoolyard fight, but I noticed that on top of a planter than housed the large tree in the lunch quad was Cisco, with a Bible in his hand and a passion in his heart. He had filled his pockets with quarters that morning and, during lunch, stood up on the planter and threw out handfuls of quarters. Now in a public school, a couple of quarters can get you a couple of snacks, which is huge for hungry, growing boys and girls. Dozens and dozens of high school kids came flocking to the scene to get free money, and Cisco simply opened up and preach a testimony of God's love and freedom. Within a few moments, on a high school public campus, nineteen teens gave their lives to the Lord. Here is someone who looked to what they had, not what they didn't. Cisco may not have had a degree in theology or experience working in ministry, but he had a history with God and a love for the lost.

The next scene in Acts chapter 3 is the fruit and joy of the church and her work:

> *So he, leaping up, stood and walked and entered the temple with them—walking, leaping, and praising God. And all the people saw him walking and praising God. Then they knew that it was he who sat begging alms at the Beautiful Gate of the temple; and they were filled with wonder and amazement at what had happened to him. (Acts 3:1–10)*

The cripple for all his life was *outside* the temple—the presence of God. His illness and condition kept him apart from the presence of God. Now we know and believe that God will never leave us or forsake us (Hebrews 13:5) and that He is always near; in fact He is closer than our skin (1 Corinthians 3:16), yet we are all too aware of the distractions that trials, pain, or sickness can bring in our lives. When we are focused on our issues and hurts, we turn our attention away from heavenward to inward.

This passage of scripture says the cripple was "walking and praising God." He was walking (physically healed) and praising God (spiritually healed) and made his way into the temple, where he would undoubtedly draw closer to the Lord and others (relationally healed). You and I have the same ability and commandment to bring the lost into the kingdom of God, where they can experience all the same things. Remember that the miracle of the cripple was just two believers on their way to church who dared to believe God at His Word and agree with heaven.

## Not Just a Building, but a Body

I share the story in Acts chapter 3 to illustrate the fact that church cannot be confined by four walls. As we saw in Peter and John and our team in Tijuana, it is possible to have church outside church. When we are walking, talking, and living the New Testament, we have come into alignment with our true identity as the bride of Christ (Revelation 19:7). An insecure person unsure of their role and identity will not find peace or joy, and it is obvious in any relationship that a loss of self-worth or identity brings forth separation. We must step into our role as ambassadors of Christ (2 Corinthians 5:20) and colaborers with the Lord (1 Corinthians 3:9) by taking risks and using the ordinary things in life to demonstrate the supernatural.

As carriers of the presence of God and His power, we cannot be paralyzed by fears and insecurity, nor can we neglect the truth of what God says we can do in and through Him. It reminds me of a lesson I learned from my mother, a woman of more action than complaint. It was a beautiful Southern California afternoon as my mother and I drove down a main street in our town in route back home. My mother had just picked me up at work as I was still a teenager at this time and was without a car of my own. The traffic was heavier that day as I had gotten out of work a couple of hours earlier than normal. The six-lane main road was busy with vehicles as we were dead center of an elementary, middle, and high school all letting out of school at the same time.

Nothing seemed out of the ordinary that day until our car was overwhelmed with a thunderous boom. My mom had yelled out, "Oh my God!" My senses went into overload, and I began frantically searching the car and mirrors for anything that had gone wrong. My mom kept repeating "Oh my God, oh my God!" as she sped up. Still in panic, I yelled out, "What?! What's the matter? What's wrong?!" As she made one of the sharpest U-turns of my life, I finally saw what had stirred her up so bad. At the bottom of the hill, there was a car flipped onto its roof. The boom we felt was the impact of a seventy-six-year-old lady who had lost control and crashed into the base of a streetlight. My mother's exclamation was a result of seeing this car literally flipping through the air. My mother was a medical assistant, volunteer firefighter, and was currently working for the sheriff's department; needless to say she had seen many sides of the road accidents and has come to the rescue of many accident victims.

We raced down the hill, where two other motorists had already parked to give assistance. My mother threw her cell phone at me and ordered, "Call 911!" I took the phone and made the call, desperately trying to keep up with my little five-foot-four-inch-tall mom, who was racing to the accident scene in her one-of-a-kind sunflower summer dress. I finished the call, and when I finally got to the scene, I saw one of the most incredible things of my life. Four large men were standing about twenty feet away from the car that had rested upside down in the bicycle lane as gasoline was pouring out of the vehicle and the engine still running. These men were too afraid to risk their lives to save another. This elderly lady was trapped upside down by her seat belt, and no one had the boldness to free her.

My mother literally plowed through the middle of those "men" and went to the rescue. The door was crushed shut, so she braced one foot against the door to attempt to rip it open. Finally these men stepped in and helped my mom pry the door open. My mother crawled on her back in shattered glass, calmed the lady down, and freed her from the seat belt while dragging her out of the wreckage, all the while supporting her neck. The accident victim was pulled to safety, and paramedics arrived on the scene shortly after. I stood in the background, doing a little dance, singing, "That's my mama!"

That day my mother shined, not because of her experience working under highly stressful situations, but because of a willingness to say yes under *any* circumstance, fear, or logic. Any person who pulled over on the side of the road that day had enough talent, strength, and logic to pull that elderly lady out of the wreckage. The only thing that separated my mother from the rest of the crowd was radical obedience. When you are radically obedient, it means that you will do what you know is right despite fear, insecurity, or at times, common sense. My mother knew the dangers of a car that could have possibly blown up. She knew the embarrassment of crawling around while wearing a dress. Her body was screaming at her, "Don't go into that car," but her mind was made up and her heart surrendered to be willing to be a *body*, not just a *building*.

When I speak of "radical obedience," I am not referring to plain old sin. The blood of Jesus was more than sufficient to cover all of our sins—past, present, and future. We live under a new covenant of grace and are no longer slaves to the law (Romans 6:14). When I say radical obedience, I am referring to the over-the-top obedience, the risk-taking obedience, and the "this doesn't make sense" obedience. You have the DNA of greatness in you and a spirit of a victor, but none of that will be released unless you say yes to God. I'm not sure about you, but when I feel as if I am not living up to my potential or walking in my destiny, I have a huge void and emptiness gnawing away on the inside.

Far too many churches have not tasted success or victory, not because they are not equipped or talented enough, but because they have limited themselves by extinguishing the fire that burns on their hearts. We reason things away, cower in fear, shut down in our insecurity, and pretend we really didn't hear what the Lord just told us. The kingdom of God does not advance with lazy, apathetic, and passive believers. The kingdom is spread by followers of Jesus who are willing to lay aside their fears, reputation, and lives to do what is right.

Left to ourselves, we would ultimately fail through our own efforts and works, but praise be to God we have not been abandoned (John 14:18). Though we may face trials of many kinds, we have a God of all power on our side, and through Him we can do anything (Genesis 18:14). While the world dies all around us, God is waiting for the saint who cries out, "Here I am, God, use me, I will go where You are going. Go and say what you saying."

We are the hope of the world, the light on the hill because we carry the answer to anything life or the devil can throw at us. Our perspective cannot be limited anymore to the finite, but we must open ourselves up to the reality that we have been chosen for such a time as this in the middle of the broad spectrum of eternity to bring heaven into this existence and lead the world into an eternal relationship with the Lord and His love.

# Chapter 7

## *Revival, Not Survival*

In 1904, God used a twenty-six-year-old coal miner from Wales to spark one of the greatest revivals in recent history. Evan Roberts was a simple man who was an apprentice to a forger but who had a strong desire to preach the Gospel. The only book he had ever read was the Bible, and it was his most prized possession. Roberts would take his Bible wherever he went, including work, where he would store it away in any nook or cranny for any opportunity to scan a few pages of the scripture that brought him so much joy and hope.

The Welsh revival spread quickly to many surrounding countries, and the accounts of what God did are not only astounding, but also tremendously inspiring. The entire country was aflame for God as churches remained open twenty-four hours a day. People stormed the churches, and every Sunday you would have to arrive early to win a seat. Others would have to stand or listen from outside. Police stations were hardly necessary. Pubs and bars were completely shut down. Sporting events were literally deserted. Purity was rising to the point that coal miners had to retrain their horses now that their foul language had been cleaned up. Tens of thousands of people were saved, and Wales was awakened to a relationship with the true God.[3]

3   *Revival: Principles to change the world.* Winkie Pratney, 1984, pg 188-189

There is just a spiritual state you can reach where your love for God is almost an obsession. When you are on a spiritual high, every decision, action, word, and prayer stems from a white-hot relationship with the Holy Spirit. Revival, to me, is when this happens to a region or country all at once. There is a divine expression and manifestation of the realities of the Father's heart and heaven. The problem is that we only see glimpses of revival, not sustained revival. There are no ups and downs in heaven, and there shouldn't be any here as well.

Part of the reason in seeing a decline of a move of God is wrong thinking. If you expect a revival or move of God to eventually come down or plateau, you will see just that. However, if you view revival as a lifestyle and true desire of what the Father wants for earth, there will be a sustained move of God that moves from glory to glory. My conviction is that the children of God were not meant for survival; we were meant for revival.

The church today is not a power source that equips and serves the people with life-transforming power and teaching. If anything, the church has taught us how to cope, deal with, and avoid the troubles of the world. To me it is simple: if we host the presence of God, the very Maker of everything in existence, we should be fully fit to handle any of and all life's troubles and worries. The church should be bringing the answer to Wall Street, the White House, and world issues such as famine, hunger, and AIDS. Believers should walk with an awareness that what we hold is more powerful than anything we will ever face in life. From the ends of the world to right in your own backyard, we should be releasing the power of Jesus all around us. Yet we lack power and influence because God's people lack revelation and risk.

As we saw with Evan Roberts and with many revivals, things can literally happen overnight. It doesn't take a superspiritual, supereducated person to be used by God to start a movement; it simply takes one person who says "Here I am, God, use me" (Isaiah 6:8). One modern-day example of someone taking a stand and releasing revival is Pastor and Senator James Meeks. Pastor Meeks leads Salem Baptist Church in Chicago, a church of over twenty thousand congregants and one of the fastest-growing churches in America. It is obvious that Pastor Meeks is not just a voice in the religious stream, but the educational and political as well. A few years back his church was able to shut down over thirty-two bars and liquor stores in their community. Not only were they reaching the unreachable by the tens of thousands, but their secular community was also affected by the power of God.[4]

We all have the power to release the power of God, but like anything breathed of the Lord, it must first begin with devotion, intimacy, and the Father's heart. Let's look at the scriptures and take account of one of my favorite revivals of the Old Testament:

*Josiah was eight years old when he became king, and he reigned in Jerusalem thirty-one years. He did what was right in the eyes of the LORD and followed the ways of his father David, not turning aside to the right or to the left.*

*In the eighth year of his reign, while he was still young, he began to seek the God of his father David. In his twelfth year he began to purge Judah and Jerusalem of high places, Asherah poles and idols.*

---

4    http://www.senatedem.ilga.gov/index.php/about-me-meeks

*Under his direction the altars of the Baals were torn down; he cut to pieces the incense altars that were above them, and smashed the Asherah poles and the idols. These he broke to pieces and scattered over the graves of those who had sacrificed to them. He burned the bones of the priests on their altars, and so he purged Judah and Jerusalem. In the towns of Manasseh, Ephraim and Simeon, as far as Naphtali, and in the ruins around them, he tore down the altars and the Asherah poles and crushed the idols to powder and cut to pieces all the incense altars throughout Israel. Then he went back to Jerusalem. In the eighteenth year of Josiah's reign, to purify the land and the temple, he sent Shaphan son of Azaliah and Maaseiah the ruler of the city, with Joah son of Joahaz, the recorder, to repair the temple of the LORD his God.*

*Then they entrusted it to the men appointed to supervise the work on the LORD's temple. These men paid the workers who repaired and restored the temple. They also gave money to the carpenters and builders to purchase dressed stone, and timber for joists and beams for the buildings that the kings of Judah had allowed to fall into ruin.*

*"I have found the Book of the Law in the house of the LORD."
And Hilkiah gave the book to Shaphan. So Shaphan carried the book to the king, bringing the king word, saying, "All that was committed to your servants they are doing. And they have gathered the money that was found in the house of the LORD, and have delivered it into the hand of the overseers and the workmen." Then Shaphan the scribe told the king, saying, "Hilkiah the priest has given me a book." And Shaphan read it before the king.*

*Thus it happened, when the king heard the words
of the Law, that he tore his clothes.*


*Then the king called together all the elders of Judah and Jerusalem.
He went up to the temple of the LORD with the people of Judah,
the inhabitants of Jerusalem, the priests and the Levites—all the
people from the least to the greatest. He read in their hearing all
the words of the Book of the Covenant, which had been found in the
temple of the LORD. The king stood by his pillar and renewed the
covenant in the presence of the LORD—to follow the LORD and
keep his commands, statutes and decrees with all his heart and all
his soul, and to obey the words of the covenant written in this book.*

*Then he had everyone in Jerusalem and Benjamin pledge
themselves to it; the people of Jerusalem did this in accordance
with the covenant of God, the God of their ancestors.*


## Releasing Personal and World Revival


### 1. Remove excuses.

Josiah came from the royal and messianic line of David. He
was already positioned for greatness simply by building off his
fathers of past generations. You may have a long line of believers
in your family or you may not. If you are so blessed as to have a
lineage of family that has passionately followed Jesus, it is wise
to build off their legacies. If you are the first believer in your
family line, have no fear because you have a great family history
in heaven. Your Heavenly *Father* has blessed you with everything

you need to be a world changer and to have change in your own life.

At a mature age of eight, Josiah took the throne. Though this may look ridiculous from today's standpoint; it wasn't all that rare in those days. Furthermore, it proves to me that the only qualification we need in order to be used by God is loving and following Him. Our reasons for not walking in the power of God are inexcusable. Though we may be young, uneducated, or have never read through the Bible, God can still use you.

Having a king of only eight years old who led God's people into one of the greatest revivals also demonstrates a childlike faith. Josiah had not been tainted by the world but rested with a dependency on a relationship with God. This passage says that he did "right in the eyes of the LORD and followed the ways of his father David." What is more impressive is that he did not "turn aside to the right or left." This means that Josiah, even at an extremely young age, *chose* to love God with all his heart and had a focus on the kingdom of God. In order to have such discipline in your life to follow God at all costs and without reserve, you must have your mind made up and *convinced* that the thing you are giving your life to is worth dying for.

We can no longer offer excuses to a Christian life in neutral. Hebrews 12:1 says, "Therefore, since we are surrounded by such a great cloud of witnesses, let us throw off everything that hinders and the sin that so easily entangles. And let us run with perseverance the race marked out for us." If the same power that rose Christ from the grave, lives in you (Romans 8:11), then you have no reason to doubt that the Lord can use you to alter the course of history.

## 2. Remove wrong influences.

In the first grade I remember the entire school being terrified of one bully. This second-grader had a condition that let him grow to an adult height at seven years old. He was literally six feet tall in the second grade. He wasn't so much of a bully as he was a *boy* who had an obvious advantage over everything.

During a small recess break on the playground one day, this bully's influence was shattered. A brave and rambunctious little kid was dared to kick the giant. This kid snuck up behind the bully and literally kicked his butt. The entire playground stopped—bouncing balls were falling in slow motion, tumbleweeds were inching across the playground, and all sound was coming to a halt. The bully turned around, and we expected his face to turn bloodred and pummel this small kid. The entire playground rushed to the scene—I mean which kid doesn't want to witness a murder? Yet the unthinkable happened. The bully's face turned red, but it was followed with tears. He grabbed his rear and ran to a noon duty and cried out, "That kid kicked me in the butt!" From that moment forward, no one was ever afraid.

In the same way that this bully's influence was removed forever on the playground, the devil's influence was forever removed from believers. However, we can still engage in sinful things and leave ourselves open to Satan's influence by surrounding ourselves with things that are contrary to the Word of God. Young king Josiah had a love for God and began to remove all the idols in the land. An idol is "an image or other material object representing a deity to which religious worship is addressed."[5] It is putting an object or idea above God's ways and having such a focus on that thought or thing that it is almost worship or is worship.

---

5   http://dictionary.reference.com/browse/idol

Josiah did not simply teach on how to remove idols or start a program where people who were struggling with "idol addiction" could go for support and help. No, with the authority given to him by God, he exercised his power and removed the idols in the land. Josiah didn't simply remove the idols or give them away to a more wicked kingdom; he destroyed them, even crushing them down to powder and defiling the bones of the old idol priests. The young king further enforced the removal of idols when he reestablished the worship of God to the kingdom.

The Bible is simple and clear on this matter, "Have no other god's before me" (Exodus 20:3). The Lord should be the priority of our lives, yet in our culture it is easy to become distracted. With social media, TV, Internet, and the simple business of life, it is easy to put God in the low end of your priorities. The Bible speaks about this danger when it says in Matthew 12:34, "For out of the abundance of the heart the mouth speaks." TV and other media are not sinful, necessarily. Movies, social media, and other things, though they may not scream "God" all the time, are not sinful in themselves yet can lead us into distraction or deception. It is known that "what you put in is what you put out." If you desire to see a change in your heart, your actions/ behaviors, or your family, be conscious and purposeful of what you are spiritually digesting. I know it is elementary teaching, but simple rules are easy to break and forget. Again it is easy to focus on behavior modification before heart transformation, yet lasting change is only a result of the positive and godly things we allow into our hearts. If it is change and breakthrough you desire, do so from the inside out, not outside in. One slogan I like to tell myself is "Stop looking for your breakthrough and start living it."

I remember a few years ago I had one of those rare moments when I was home alone. My son was in school, my wife was running errands, and I had a day off. I looked around the house and noticed that our busy week had become obvious by the mess in the house. Dishes and laundry were piling up, and toys were laid out all over the house. With my humble and extremely godly self, I decided I would bless my wife and do some cleaning. I grabbed load after load of laundry (one of the chores she hates the most) and began to wash, dry, and fold. I noticed a wonderful joy that rose up in me. If you have ever sacrificed and given to someone else, you feel extremely good about yourself. I felt like a great husband, felt like a sacrificial father, and a believer who was exercising what a humble servant was all about.

My wife had come home, and I sat on the couch, reading, pretending like I had done nothing all day. It is one thing to do something for someone when they *know* you are going to do it; it is another completely when you catch them off guard. As I sat there pretending to read, I was waiting at any moment for the exclamation of thanks I would get. Yet minute by slow minute passed by, and I heard nothing. Finally I got up and asked, "Babe, did you notice anything different about the house?" She said, "Uh, no, why?" I very calmly and proudly said, "Oh, nothing, I just did, like, six loads of laundry for you." She looked puzzled and said, "You mean those ones over there?" I said, "Yup!" She continued, "You mean the clothes I already washed?" Let's just say my bubble was popped.

I had spent all this effort and all my day off trying to clean something that was already clean! Unfortunately, this is exactly how we tend to live today. We have already been cleansed of our sins but live as sinners. We have been given every spiritual blessing yet live as if we have been forgotten. We beg and plead for victory and breakthrough when Christ has already defeated the grave, the devil, sin, sickness, and sorrow. It is time to stop looking for our breakthrough and start living it!

The Lord has given us everything that we need in life and more power than I believe we fully understand. Though God has supplied us with all things, nothing will happen in our lives if we are not purposefully releasing His truth into our lives and circumstances. Transformation comes by the renewing of our minds (Romans 12:2). When our minds are in alignment with the truth of our identity and the promise God has given us, we can then be in position to *release* what He has given us. You cannot give away what you don't have, and you cannot release what you don't understand. The first step in having a greater awareness of the power of God and revival in your heart and world is to remove the wrong influences. Remove those things that want to take God's place in your life. Pastor Joseph Price puts it this way, "We don't fight *for* victory, we fight *from* victory." We are not fighting to receive our breakthrough; we are fighting to keep the influence of Satan away from our breakthrough.

## 3. Remove separation.

After King Josiah established God as his priority and removed the idols of the land, the next thing he did was send workers to repair the temple of God. In the Old Testament, God was not indwelling in every believer. His very presence was in the tabernacle or temple where the Ark of the Covenant of God rested (Exodus 25:22). So in essence, to restore the "church" or temple (place of worship) was to once again lead people into the very presence of God. In the same way the priest of the Old Testament found the answers for everything in life in the presence of God, you and I must move, speak, and act from the presence of God (more on the presence in chapter 9). The other important truth about reestablishing the church was its culture and communal benefits.

I gave my life to the Lord at the age of fifteen. I began attending a youth group at a local church that also had a Christian private school. Due to the large campus and heavy foot traffic, the church hired a weekend crew of high school students to take care of the facilities after all services. What better labor than that of teenagers. Three months after I gave my life to the Lord, I asked my youth pastor if there were any openings on the team. He initially got me hired, and I was thrilled to have my first real job and to work alongside eight other friends who were also in my youth group. Every weekend we got together to clean the church and set up different areas of the church for the weekend services. We planned the children's ministry, the patio and food setup, and made sure the place was immaculate. Though we had a job to do, we were also teenagers, and I had some of the greatest laughs and memories while on staff of a church's maintenance department.

The team was not only together for the eight hours of work on the weekends; we were literally together whenever possible. We went to youth group together on Wednesdays and all three services on the weekends; we served together, went to Bible study together, went to the movies and Denny's restaurant on Friday nights together. This wonderful group of friends allowed me to live in a culture of God. It kept me out of trouble, and my boys held me to accountability in what I was confessing. Our group of friends was a young "church" in action. Many can testify to the joy of having a group of friends you grew up in the church with and the benefits and wonderful memories it brought you.

When King Josiah reestablished the temple, he wasn't just putting a church back in the region; he shifted the culture and changed the motives and desires of the nation. The church has changed over the centuries, but the powerful truth remains that we must create places of worship that honor the presence of God and allow the people of the church to have an avenue of freedom and relationship. We cannot be so focused on numbers, programs, and formulas that we miss out on power, relationship, and the presence of God. Churches today in whatever denomination, style, or program must give way for the presence of God and allow freedom at the altars. Though the Lord may bless with wonderful structures, buildings, and technology, if the first thing that people notice is the building above His presence, there is something wrong. When the people of the church are testifying to a strong, manifest presence of the Lord, healthy relationships, and a release of the power of God, we are doing something right. Tactics and intelligence are mere tools of the church, but it is honor and the presence of God that will change the church.

## 4. Remove ignorance of God's Word.

The scriptures were found in the ruins of the temple and read aloud to King Josiah. The Scripture says in verse 19 that Josiah "tore his clothes" at the hearing of the Word of God. In the Bible, whenever someone would tear their clothes or garment, it was a sign of distress or mourning, signifying that you are undone or broken. When Josiah heard the words of the law, he was broken, knowing that he had failed to hear the Word of the Lord and it did not match the life he was living. When we read the scripture, we must ask ourselves if our lives line up with those of the heroes and stories of the Bible. Are we living out the promises that God has spoken to us through His Word and sacrifice of His Son?

There are several things that can cause us to have a wrong perspective on the Word of God or to reason away its original meaning. One of the things that hinder the effect of God's Word in our lives is man's traditions and religion. I don't want to pull the religion card and start bashing everyone who does not walk in the supernatural or believe in the baptism of the Holy Spirit and tongues. I don't feel the need to label and seclude myself from people who don't agree with the things I agree with. This causes separation in the church, and heavy debate can lead to ill intent. I simply want to point out that our man-made formulas, religion, and tradition can get in the way of applying the scriptures to our lives in their full effect. The Bible says in Mark 7:13, "Making the word of God of no effect through your tradition which you have handed down. And many such things you do." We have to be careful that we are not looking more at the intelligence of the church, instead of looking at the power and truth of the Bible. We cannot reason away or dismiss something in God's Word that we are uncomfortable with. Many men are guilty (whether intentional or unintentional) of creating theories or doctrines that nullify the Word of God. If we read a command from the Lord that we know will lead us away from our comfort zone, we must not dismiss it or ignore it but trust that God will only lead us through something that we are already equipped to handle. Rather than flee from truth, receive the power God has given you and place your trust in a god who will lead you to greater victory in your life.

Another way of ignoring the power of God's written word is to get into the teaching trap. Millions of churches are professional Bible institutions. If you want to learn about God's Word, you don't have to go very far. We have Bible-teaching churches by the dozens per street. There are Bible colleges galore, and every

Bible study resource known to man is on the Internet—even on our phones. All these are great, and every believer must pour into Bible study and understanding the scriptures for themselves, but we must never fall into the trap of simply learning about the scriptures but never doing anything with it. The Bible says in James 1:22 that we must be "doers of the Word not just hearers." Paul even said in Romans 15:19, "In mighty signs and wonders, by the power of the Spirit of God, so that from Jerusalem and round about to Illyricum I have **fully** preached the gospel of Christ" (emphasis mine). In the New Testament, the Word of God was fully preached when it was fully demonstrated and released.

Our lives should be a testimony to others of the power of God's Word. We benefit so much for the discipline of studying and apply the scriptures. Psalm 1:3 says, "He shall be like a tree Planted by the rivers of water, that brings forth its fruit in its season, whose leaf also shall **not wither**; and whatever he does shall **prosper**" (emphasis mine). We have a promise that there is more success, protection, and power for those who hide the Word of God in their heart. We cannot expect to see victory if we are not seeing God's Word in action in our lives. Faith comes from the hearing and hearing the Word of God (Romans 10:17), we are blessed when we hear and keep the Word (Luke 11:28), and we have been commanded that we shall not "live on bread alone but by every word of God" (Luke 4:4).

King Josiah led the people to the power of God through the power of the scripture. It says in verse 31 that the king "renewed the Covenant." Josiah reestablished God's original promise for the Israelites. He brought the people back to the promise of the land and the truth of their identity. When this was done, the people were able to experience revival and also *maintain* it. That entire generation walked and lived in the power and truth of God's Word. You and I must experience the same.

## Giving Up Everything to Receive It All

I am greatly inspired by the recent convictions and actions of Pastor Francis Chan. Pastor Chan was the senior pastor of Cornerstone Church in Simi Valley, California, and author of *Crazy Love* and *Forgotten God*. He is a highly sought-after speaker and extremely successful in the eyes of millions of believers. For some pastors, Francis Chan is living the dream. But in 2010 he decided to follow a call and stirring in his heart. To the shock of the Christian world, he resigned as senior pastor of Cornerstone, "sold all his possessions," and followed the voice of Jesus. He said that he didn't know where God was leading him but for the time being wanted to be around people who are living examples of the New Testament model. So Francis and his family took off to visit countries, such as India and China.

One night after church, I went home and decided to listen to a sermon on my computer (I guess this is what pastors are supposed to do in their free time). I stumbled on a video of a sermon by Francis titled "Radically Following Jesus."[6] In this sermon he describes again the calling God placed on his heart and began to share some of the stories from his overseas missions. He was overwhelmed at the stories these Christians had in countries where Christianity is illegal. Stories of people being beaten to death, excommunicated, and murdered.

One of the stories has captured my attention, and the impact <u>has burned on</u> the memory of my heart. Francis gave an account

6    http://www.youtube.com/watch?v=ogRJHOr5fEo

of a bus driver's testimony. At age eleven, this bus driver told his father he had given his life to Jesus. The father commanded him never to refer to him as father again, gathered the boy's things, and kicked him out in the mud and pouring rain. The boy had been on his own ever since. Francis (like many of us) couldn't believe or comprehend the devotion. The bus driver looked surprised and said, "Why are you so shocked?" Francis replied with "I'm just amazed at your story." The bus driver gave a sobering reply, "Isn't this every believer's story?" Francis elaborated that in America things are much different. In the United States you have "these buildings called churches with music and a speaker. And if you don't like the speaker, you can go down the street to another church and look for a better speaker." Francis, in bewilderment, said, "I just don't understand how you can be so devoted." The bus driver then said something that made me drop the bowl of popcorn I had been eating. He said, "Well, when you are forced to give up *everything*, how can you not be fully committed?"

Those words will remain with me for a long time. America has yet to see the manifestation of love, power, and grace that the Lord has been wanting to release. We must remember that we are not designed for survival. Our spirits were wired for revival. We can be the generation that changes it all, like the first-century believers. We can be the mark in history when it all went back to God's original desire.

# Chapter 8

## *Invisible God*

A FEW YEARS AGO I took a few friends and volunteers up to a conference that had a focus on worship and the supernatural. Coming from a nondenominational background and even an Assemblies of God background, I still wasn't prepared for what I saw, experienced, and enjoyed. The place was filled with thousands of young people who came for one purpose: loving God. I had been to every conference, special event, and Christian camp under the sun and had never seen anything like it. There were no games, no prizes, no funny videos, no attractions; it was literally four- to five-hour services of nothing but intense musical worship, teaching, and prayer. People were praying for other people. Bodies were on the floor under the power of God. The energy in the room felt as if 100 percent of the people in attendance were focused and engaged in worship.

Toward the end of one of the nighttime sessions, a guest speaker who is known for prayer and fasting movements went onstage to give the message. He stepped onstage after an hour and a half of worship and what I can only describe as "heaven coming down to kiss us." Toward the end of the sermon, the speaker began telling a story of the impact of the song "I Exalt Thee" decades ago. He led the group in a cappella worship, and the electricity hit the place once again. The power in the room was as if it were being rattled by a 7.0-magnitude earthquake.

You could see in the expression on the face of the speaker and the volunteers of the event that they were unsure of where to go next. This was something special.

The speaker simply could not get back into the sermon to wrap things up. The crowd kept going, louder and louder, more and more passionate. It was one of the moments where I thanked God and thought, *I am standing in a place where revival is being birthed.* It was like a little kid blowing up a large balloon and not stopping. At any moment the balloon would burst, and you stand there bracing yourself for the impact. I stood there wondering where this was all gonna go. Sadly, the speaker felt called by God to lead us into a forty-day fast. My heart broke. Here you have an auditorium full of on-fire young people crying out for more of God, and we are led into a fast? I have nothing against fasting, but wasn't that moment at that conference what we would all fast for! By the end of the night, we were kicked out as the volunteers had to shut down the facility, and we took our "nighttime revival" out to the streets.

After moments like the one from this story, I can't help but wonder how many great moves of God never had a chance to launch. We hope, cry out, and pray for mighty "moves of God" and the "more of God," yet when our prayers are answered, we don't know where to go with it. Sadly, many in the body of Christ today have no idea how to handle victory and breakthrough when it comes. Like the speaker who went back into fasting, we resort to the fundamental and elementary things of our faith and stay on the toddler stages of our relationship with God because our hearts are not properly prepared to into the next level of glory.

First Corinthians 4:20 says, "For the kingdom of God *is* not in word but in power." You can go to any church today and find wonderful biblical teaching, but there are only pockets of believers who are genuinely and properly stewarding God's *power*. The reason, in my opinion, why we are not seeing the miraculous, supernatural, and power of God in our churches, homes, and hearts is due to the fact that we have an awkward and ignorant relationship with the *Power Giver*, the Holy Spirit.

When teaching or studying on the Holy Spirit, there is often a heavy debate. There are hefty disagreements on the role of the Holy Spirit in the life of the believer, whether or not gifts are for today or reserved only for the first church, and that of the baptism of the Holy Spirit. One of the main reasons, in my opinion, is that the influence and ministry of the Holy Spirit in the believer's life will naturally draw you to the power of God and greater depths in your relationship with the Father. This is uncharted and scary territory for many Christians, and for that reason, whatever is unexplainable or void in the believer's life is ultimately excused away or labeled as heresy and of the occult. It is easy to remain in lack or struggle because as Christians, we know how to handle that. We can put up with stress, struggle, and hardships, but are we really prepared to receive and walk in the victory we have always prayed about? The bottom line and main encouragement for me is that fact that Jesus couldn't operate apart from the Holy Spirit and neither should I.

Though it is true that there are some who may abuse the grace and freedom in the Holy Spirit or operate in the gifts for the sole intent on greed, we cannot be deterred in our pursuit of the more of God based on the poor stewardship of others. Whether you are an overdramatic charismatic or conservative, we *all* have a command from Jesus to walk in the power of the Holy Spirit and to do the things that He did while on earth (Matthew 6:10, John 14:12). We cannot avoid the Spirit in an attempt to avoid the responsibility of releasing heaven on earth and living a "more than conqueror life." We cannot let out insecurity and wrong perspective of our identity keep us from the ministry of the Holy Spirit. We cannot afford in this day and age to allow the unknown and fear, convince us to live apart from the power of the Spirit.

## *Who Is the Holy Spirit?*

As I mentioned earlier, I was saved at a nondenominational church where the Holy Spirit wasn't taught much, nor did we walk in the gifts of the Spirit. It was a seeker-sensitive environment, so they did not deny the power of God, but they didn't walk in it either. At that time in my life I felt that if the Holy Spirit were invisible from our ministry and church. He must be silent as well. Though He was referenced and mentioned whenever someone experienced a good feeling in worship or finding strength in a difficult time, I had no idea who He was.

There are a lot of misconceptions in the church about the Holy Spirit. Many view Him as a Holy "Ghost" much like Casper the Friendly Ghost. Some have viewed Him as a force or a feeling. Others go to the other extreme and view Him almost like a mother looking over your shoulder, ready to condemn and convict you of every little thing you do wrong. The Holy Spirit is neither of those things and can be experienced as genuine and real as the Son and Father.

When I was in Bible college, I took a class on the Holy Spirit, and on the first night of class, my professor announced, "The Holy Spirit is a person with a personality." Obviously this rocked my world right from the start. The professor went on to say, "He has a personality. You can talk and pray to Him. He is not an 'it.'" The Holy Spirit can speak to you and bless you with different things." One of the first things we must understand is that the Holy Spirit is God, an equal of the Trinity: Father, Son, and Holy Spirit. He is all-powerful as it says in Luke 1:35:

*And the angel answered and said to her, "The Holy Spirit will come upon you, and the power of the Highest will overshadow you; therefore, also, that Holy One who is to be born will be called the Son of God."*

*The Holy Spirit is omnipresent, meaning everywhere at one time, as we see clearly in Psalm 139:7, "Where can I go from Your Spirit? Or where can I flee from Your presence?" He is also eternal (Hebrews 9:14), and we see Him even in the first chapter of the Bible, Genesis 1:*

*In the beginning God created the heavens and the earth. The earth was without form, and void; and darkness was on the face of the deep. And the Spirit of God was hovering over the face of the waters. Then God said. (Genesis 1:1–3)*

I love how the scripture opens with a glimpse of the Godhead right from the beginning. The scripture here says, "In the beginning *God*." Here we see God the Father. In verse 3 we see that "God *spoke*." We know from John chapter 1 that Jesus was "the Word and the Word was with God and the Word was God"; therefore, we see God the Son in creation. Lastly, verse 2 states that the "*Spirit*" was hovering over the creation. Herein we see the Holy Spirit as part of the Godhead and in equality as God.

## *Ministry of the Spirit*

I have not tried this, but I can almost guarantee that if you were to take a survey with one hundred Bible-believing Christians, what they thought the Holy Spirit does in their lives, most would say, "Convict me of sin." The Holy Spirit in the Christian world has been treated like your conscience, constantly letting you know what you are doing wrong. The scripture says in John 16:8 that the Holy Spirit will "convict the *world* of sin." I am a believer and a citizen of heaven; therefore, I count myself out as being numbered of "the world." The Holy Spirit will impress an unbeliever of their need of Jesus the Savior, but we clearly know our sin and don't need an eternal God to point that out. It does not take a prophet or man of God to point out our flaws. I think we are pretty aware of them already! Furthermore, John 3:17 says, "For God did not send His Son into the world to condemn the world, but that the world through Him might be saved." The Spirit is more than God's cosmic hallway monitor. He is God and He lives in you and me (1 Corinthians 3:16).

The primary purpose of the role of the Holy Spirit in our lives is *power*. In Acts 1:8 it says, "But you shall receive power when the Holy Spirit has come upon you." The word in the Greek, *dunamis*, is where we get the word *dynamite* from. This word for us is the same word used for Jesus in Luke 4:14, "Then Jesus returned in the power of the Spirit to Galilee." Jesus operated under the power and ministry of the Holy Spirit:

*How God anointed Jesus of Nazareth with the Holy Spirit and with power, who went about doing good and healing all who were oppressed by the devil, for God was with Him.*

(*Acts 10:38*)

The apostle Paul knew very well the power of the Holy Spirit:

> *Now may the God of hope fill you with all joy and peace in believing, that you may abound in hope by the power of the Holy Spirit. (Romans 15:13)*

> *In mighty signs and wonders, by the **power** of the **Spirit** of God, so that from Jerusalem and round about to Illyricum I have fully preached the gospel of Christ. (Romans 15:19)*

Apart from being the source of God's power in our lives, the scriptures say we can receive Him as our guide in truth as it says in John 16:13, "However, when He, the Spirit of truth, has come, He will guide you into all truth." He is known as our helper in John 14:16, "And I will pray the Father, and He will give you another Helper, that He may abide with you forever." We also have promises of the Holy Spirit being our teacher and giving us the things we need to say:

> *Now we have received, not the spirit of the world, but the Spirit who is from God, that we might know the things that have been freely given to us by God. These things we also speak, not in words which man's wisdom teaches but which the Holy Spirit teaches. (1 Corinthians 2:12–13)*

*But when they arrest you and deliver you up, do not worry beforehand, or premeditate what you will speak. But whatever is given you in that hour, speak that; for it is not you who speak, but the Holy Spirit. (Mark 13:11)*

In my own, personal life, I struggled for years with low self-esteem and the wrong perspective of my identity. I lived insecure and doubted what God could be in my life until I surrendered to the power of the Holy Spirit. Only under the revelation of all that I have in Christ could I begin to walk with confidence and boldness when facing my circumstances. The scriptures tell us:

+ We have freedom in the Spirit (Romans 8:15–16).

+ The Holy Spirit intercedes on our behalf (Romans 8:2, 27).

+ We have a Helper in our times of need (John 16:7).

+ We have confidence in knowing we have the wisdom of God at our side (Ephesians 1:17).

+ We have been grafted into God's family by the spirit of adoption (Romans 8:15).

Jesus received the words from the Father that He was a "Beloved Son," then the Holy Spirit came upon Him and Jesus began His ministry. You and I must be secure in our identity and position ourselves to be filled of the Spirit that we may walk in a greater understanding of God and flow in the power of God.

## *Benefits of the Holy Spirit*

*Bless the LORD, O my soul, And forget not
all His benefits. —Psalm 103:2*

When I was nineteen years old, I was working at my church as an interim youth pastor. One day I received a phone call from the senior pastor's assistant. She said, "Pastor has a memorial service this Friday night and can't make it, could you cover for him?" I had never done a wedding, a funeral, or even a baby dedication. She assured me that it was a ninety-four-year-old lady and that there would only be four or five family members there and simply needed a "pastor" to be available to pray. I thought to myself, *I know how to pray. How hard can this be?* I said yes to the invitation, and that Friday afternoon I suited up and made my way to Eternal Hills Chapel and Cemetery.

The service was to begin at 6:00 PM. and I arrived early at around 5:40 PM. When I walked into the chapel, it was a standing room only. There had to have been over 150 people with a full-on open casket and flowers! I was in a state of shock when the son-in-law of the deceased came running up to me. He said, "I didn't know all these people were showing up! Could you possibly come up with something and put together a small service for us?" Me and my young faith said, "Sure, I guess."

I sat on the side of the chapel and silently prayed, "Oh, Lord, I have no idea what I am doing. Holy Spirit, would you guide me and fill my mouth of Your words?" Then 6:00 PM came and I took the microphone and led an hour service flawlessly. It was a miracle. It was the Holy Spirit teaching me what to say.

As the Helper, the Holy Spirit dwells within us and guides us through the various things we face in life with the awareness of the gift and power of God that is available. We have already established that we need not look for our breakthrough but simply walk in it. One of the main tools to maintain our freedom is guarding our thoughts and staying focused on God's truth. If this is the case, the Holy Spirit is critical in our growth, as He is the Teacher and Guide. The Bible says that we must "bring every thought into captivity to the obedience of Christ" (2 Corinthians 10:5). We must remember the benefit of leaning on the Holy Spirit to guide our thoughts and fill us with the revelation of who Jesus is.

A second critical aspect of renewing the mind is standing on the Word of God. Second Timothy 3:16 says, "All Scripture *is* given by inspiration of God, and *is* profitable for doctrine, for reproof, for correction, for instruction in righteousness." We know the scriptures to be inspired by the Holy Spirit, so we must turn to the Holy Spirit in our time of study. In today's culture there is so much technology and resources available for Bible study. We have online resources, cell phone apps, and books galore, but we must never forget to gain the most from the scriptures from the One who inspired them. I believe it was Smith Wigglesworth that said, "Some read their Bible in the Hebrew or Greek, I read mine in the Holy Ghost!"

Jesus spoke of the power and benefit of the Holy Spirit in John 16:7:

*Nevertheless I tell you the truth. It is to your advantage that I go away; for if I do not go away, the Helper will not come to you; but if I depart, I will send Him to you.*

Jesus said that though His physical presence may have been a benefit to them, a greater benefit would come after He ascended to heaven, the Holy Spirit. Today so many believers are still envious of a physical Jesus on earth, rather than the unseen God who lives and dwells in our hearts.

## Baptism of the Spirit

The baptism of the Holy Spirit is a much debated topic and has been for centuries. To make the issue a little more difficult, there is a wide range of thoughts and opinions on the matter as well. If you were to do an average search of the baptism of the Holy Spirit and devote time to digging up truth for yourself, you might end up more confused than when you first started. Almost every church has a section in their bulletin or website that states what they believe, and you will find a variety of answers to the question, What is the baptism of the Holy Spirit? In regard to this question, I like to keep things simple in the same way I like to keep my walk with the Lord simple.

When we give our lives to the Lord and receive Him as Savior, we become a new creation and our past lives are gone (2 Corinthians 5:17). We are also given the promised Holy Spirit upon our salvation. Every believer who gives their lives to the Lord is blessed with the indwelling Holy Spirit as we see promised in the prophecy in Joel 2:

*And afterward, I will pour out my **Spirit** on all people. Your sons and daughters will prophesy, your old men will dream dreams, your young men will see visions. (Joel 2:28)*

Yet there is a separate experience apart from salvation with the Holy Spirit, called the baptism of the Holy Spirit. Take a look at the commandment to the disciples in Acts chapters 1 and 8:

> *And being assembled together with them, He commanded them not to depart from Jerusalem, but to wait for the Promise of the Father, "which," He said, "you have heard from Me; for John truly baptized with water, but you shall be baptized with the Holy Spirit not many days from now."*

> *Who, when they had come down, prayed for them that they might receive the Holy Spirit. For as yet He had fallen upon none of them. They had only been baptized in the name of the Lord Jesus. (Acts 8:15–16)*

One thing to notice in these passages is that Jesus didn't treat them lightly. He commanded and told us to receive the gift and baptism of the Holy Spirit. It wasn't much of an option as it is a necessity. The times we live in now are dark, and there is a need of a generation to rise and take their place of authority over the land and release the power of God. It is far too easy to become distracted, fearful, tempted, and so forth, but the blessing of the baptism of the Holy Spirit brings power, revelation, wisdom, and guidance that we may fully step into all that the Lord has called us to be.

Again my desire is to keep things simple, if you desire to be baptized of the Spirit:

## A. Ask for it.

*For everyone who asks receives; the one who seeks finds; and to the one who knocks, the door will be opened. (Luke 11:10)*

## B. Pray and Receive

*Father, I thank you for the gift of the promised Holy Spirit, and I desire the power that comes from being baptized in the Holy Spirit. I ask now, Lord, that you fill me of Your Spirit and anoint me with power from on high. Thank you for the wonderful gift, and with a glad and sincere heart, I receive all that you have for me. In Jesus's name I pray, amen.*

The biblical pattern of the baptism of the Holy Spirit is followed by speaking in tongues. I want to be sensitive to the readers who disagree with me on this belief, yet I feel led to give reason for my stance. The scriptures show different accounts of speaking in tongues following the filling of the Spirit:

*All of them were filled with the Holy Spirit and began to speak in other tongues as the Spirit enabled them. (Acts 2:4)*

*While Peter was still speaking these words, the Holy*
*Spirit came on all who heard the message. Acts 10:44*

Speaking in tongues is simply an unknown language that you pray from your spirit that God can understand. Your mind may not comprehend it, but your spirit can wrap around it as 1 Corinthians 14:14 says, "For if I pray in a tongue, my spirit prays, but my understanding is unfruitful." It is specifically catered for the edification of the believer as it says in Jude 1:20, "But you, dear friends, by building yourselves up in your most holy faith and praying in the Holy Spirit."

The gift of tongues is for all people, and the benefits are tremendous. One of the examples is found in the famous scripture about the armor of God. Though many of us know about the "helmet of salvation," "belt of truth" and so forth, many of us forget that one of the only offensive weapons we are given is *praying in the Spirit*:

*And take the helmet of salvation, and the sword of the Spirit,*
*which is the word of God; praying always with all prayer*
*and supplication in the Spirit. (Ephesians 6:17–18a)*

The gift of tongues is a wonderful and extremely edifying advantage for the believer. If you desire the gift of tongues, ask the Lord and receive from Him. I would encourage you to seek further study and discipleship from your pastor to have all your questions met.

## A God Closer Than Your Skin

My wife and I were blessed with over three hundred people at our wedding. Most people would agree that the greatest part of your wedding is when it is finally over! All the planning, stress, and chaos make driving away to the honeymoon that much sweeter. Though planning a wedding of that caliber was quite a task, we had tremendous help from dozens of family members and friends, and we could barely stand the fact that we had a roomful of presents to go home to. The excitement of hundreds of gifts was too much for us to bear, and we ended up leaving our honeymoon two days early to get home and begin the joyous process of unwrapping, returning, and purchasing all sorts of things for our new apartment and our new life together.

We got all kinds of things, including the normal eight blenders, twelve crock pots, and five toasters that every newlywed couple gets. But my most prized gift of all was a personalized Starbucks Coffee basket. A friend and coworker had purchased a decorative basket and went to a local Starbucks where she collected and purchased two coffee mugs, a pound of Christmas blend (we were married in November), a grinder, after-coffee mints, and several accessories.

I was not a coffee drinker before this gift, but one morning I decided to go through the process and see what all the fuss was about. My wife was asleep, as I am quite a morning person. The sun had just risen, and we had these amazing large portrait-style windows in our apartment. I stood in my living room and just thanked God for what he had given me. I had a new bride and stood in the middle of the room where everything was brand-new. The TV, the sofas, our furniture, and so forth were right out of the box. So I made my way to the kitchen, ground the beans, and brewed myself a pot of Christmas blend. While my brand-new coffeemaker was at work for the first time, I sat down on my new sofa to begin reading in my new Parallel Bible. I grabbed a cup of coffee as it had finished brewing, sat back down, took a sip, and . . . talk about heaven coming to earth!

That morning began a routine that I hold to this day. One of the greatest things that I look forward to at the beginning and end of the day is spending time with and learning from the Lord. I love what 1 Corinthians 13:14 says about our intimacy with the Lord:

*The grace of the Lord Jesus Christ, and the love of God, and the communion of the Holy Spirit be with you all. Amen.*

The word *communion* in this verse communicates "the presence." The birthing place for revival and an awakening to the power of God in our lives and nation rests in the truth that we must become intimate with the Lord. The Holy Spirit, God Himself being closer than our skin, has gone above and beyond to demonstrate His love for us and welcome us into His presence. When your heart is captured by God, you can then go to capture the nations.

Regardless of your belief or stance on the power, ministry, and fruit of the Spirit, one thing is certain—Jesus and His disciples relied on the Spirit to alter the course of history forever. Every great revivalist and man or woman of God had, in some way, a powerful encounter and fellowship with the Holy Spirit. We cannot afford to go one day treating the Spirit as an invisible God.

*The Spirit of the Lord is on me, because he has anointed me to proclaim good news to the poor. He has sent me to proclaim freedom for the prisoners and recovery of sight for the blind, to set the oppressed free, to proclaim the year of the Lord's favor. (Luke 4:18–19)*

# Chapter 9

## Go!

### *Holding Nothing Back*

IT WAS VERY RARE WHEN I paid attention to what was being taught in high school. My mom thinks I was a bad student who didn't apply myself. I look back now and believe that the reason I did so bad in high school was because they didn't teach Bible. I did very well in Bible college.

There was one season in my four years of high school where not only did the subject have my attention, but it also had my heart. It was my senior-year history class, and we had moved into learning about the civil rights movement. There is just something about an oppressed generation that unites with love to change a culture, to change history that engages my heart and passion. They were kicked out of schools, murdered, beaten, bitten by police dogs, injured by powerful fire hoses, yet they prevailed.

In 1968 Martin Luther King delivered a speech known now as the "I've been to the mountaintop" address. It was almost prophetic as King was assassinated shortly after delivering that message. Many highlight the portion of that speech where King speaks about "not entering the Promised Land with his followers," but this past week as the Lord led me to look back and reread that famous speech, something else jumped out at me:

*We aren't going to let any mace stop us. We are masters in our nonviolent movement in disarming police forces; they don't know what to do. I've seen them so often. I remember in Birmingham, Alabama, when we were in that majestic struggle there, we would move out of the 16th Street Baptist Church day after day; by the hundreds we would move out. And Bull Connor would tell them to send the dogs forth, and they did come; but we just went before the dogs singing, "Ain't gonna let nobody turn me around."*

*Bull Connor next would say, "Turn the fire hoses on." And as I said to you the other night, Bull Connor didn't know history. He knew a kind of physics that somehow didn't relate to the transphysics that we knew about. And that was the fact that there was a certain kind of fire that no water could put out. And we went before the fire hoses; we had known water.*

*And we just went on before the dogs and we would look at them; and we'd go on before the water hoses and we would look at it, and we'd just go on singing "Over my head I see freedom in the air."*

*(Martin Luther King, "I've been to the mountaintop" address)*

Why were tens of thousands of people able to endure such oppression and hatred? Because they were a people of promise, and people who are given a hope and promise will rise with power and determination. In our country, the declaration has been said, "All men are created equal." Martin Luther King said, in all the oppression they would sing the song "Over my head I see freedom in the air." That song was an old slave song originally titled "Over my head I see trouble in the air."

Typical civil rights marchers would meet at churches, worship God, march, and then those who weren't arrested or sent to the hospital would go back to the church and worship God again. One day a lady (don't know her name) was leading worship on a return from a march. As the choir began singing the song, she knew she was supposed to sing "Trouble in the air," but something inside her spirit wouldn't agree with it, and she made a split-second decision to sing a declaration instead. So she changed it and said, "Over my head I see *freedom* in the air." In those old-school churches, if you changed or added a chorus, the church would either sing along with you or they would stay quiet—if they didn't like the song, they stayed quiet. But as she sang, everyone began to sing along. She could almost see her great-grandparents singing this song as slaves and knowing she had a promise that one day they would all be "free at last."[7]

This is my observation: back in the '60s there was a generation that was free on the inside but oppressed on the outside. I believe today we are a generation that is free on the outside yet we have become enslaved on the inside. You see, like the generation of the civil rights movement, we too are a people of promise. We have a God who has died to show His love to us and free us of every sin, infirmity, addiction, and problem. Psalm 84:11b says, "No good thing will the Lord withhold from those who walk upright." God has given each one of us tremendous promise. We have amazing destiny and potential. We have the answer to every world issue and the power to change history for the glory of God. If that weren't enough, we live in a free country where we have the freedom to worship our God as we please

---

7    http://www.kimandreggie.com/

and have millions of biblical resources literally at our fingertips. We are so free on the outside, but so many of us are enslaved to our sin and addiction. So many of us are living in despair and depression. Many of us though we sit in a pew every Sunday are still battling hopelessness, feeling miles away from our potential and destiny.

If God has not withheld any good thing and has provided all that we need, if we live in a free country with plenty of opportunity and resources, what is the problem? Why are we finding ourselves in our own, self-made prisons? The Bible says in Jeremiah 5:25 that "your iniquities have turned these away and your sins have withheld good from you." Basically, we do it to ourselves. We through our own free will and rebellion reap the consequence of our actions and live in a self-sabotaging condition. But despite the fruit of our flesh and lusts of our hearts, we have joy because we have hope that we can align ourselves back to freedom and truth.

The Bible says in Deuteronomy 6, "Love the Lord with all your heart, soul and with all your strength." God since the beginning of time has said, "Love Me and don't hold back." It is my belief that the key to living fully surrendered to God is to live with the promise in mind, a promise that the realities of heaven are available for you and I—today.

We must fix our thoughts and minds once again on what God has given us, what He has said about us, and what the Bible says we can do. You see, we have gone from being a people of promise to a people of distraction. We listen to the media, the critics, the hurtful words of those closest to us, and without even realizing it, God's voice has become smaller and smaller and the voices of distraction are screaming in our ears, "You better find something to fix your problems."

If we cannot learn to be a people of promise who have built a trust and intimate relationship with the Lord, we will become stagnant believers and fail to see what our hearts have always dreamed about.

## *Cultivating Trust*

My favorite example of a person who developed a close relationship and trust with the Lord was the account of Abraham. Through situations that looked ludicrous and tests that most men would buckle under, Abraham stood as a man of faith and left us a legacy to be admired and followed. Look with me in the passage found in Genesis 22:

> *Now it came to pass after these things that God tested Abraham,*
> *and said to him, "Abraham!"*
> *And he said, "Here I am." Then He said, "Take now your*
> *son, your only son Isaac, whom you love, and go to the*
> *land of Moriah, and offer him there as a burnt offering*
> *on one of the mountains of which I shall tell you."*

God had called Abraham to leave his homeland and go to a foreign place to become the first of God's chosen people (Genesis 12:1). Without hesitation, Abraham trusted in the Lord, packed up his things, and took off for the land of Canaan—the future Promised Land. Though Abraham's wife, Sarah, was barren, God, in Genesis chapter 15, promised him children. The scripture says that Abraham "believed God" (Genesis 15:6) or "trusted God." Because of a promise and a trust that Abraham had with the Lord, Abraham was willing to go anyplace, to any extent, and to fulfill any call, even the most horrible of commands—kill your only child.

God had finally blessed Abraham with a child, even in his old age. After all that Abraham had gone through and the faithful life he lived, God gave him a command that felt out of the ordinary. Abraham's response is more shocking than the command:

*So Abraham rose early in the morning and saddled his donkey, and took two of his young men with him, and Isaac his son; and he split the wood for the burnt offering, and arose and went to the place of which God had told him.*

There must have been a strong and deep history between God and Abraham. To hear a command like that and to not hesitate is more than amazing. The scripture says that Abraham "rose early in the morning." If there was ever a time I would hesitate and put up excuses, it would be now! But a crazy trust allowed Abraham to endure a crazy test.

*Then on the third day Abraham lifted his eyes and saw the place afar off. And Abraham said to his young men, "Stay here with the donkey; the lad and I will go yonder and worship, and we will come back to you."*

It is one thing to have trust; it is another to stay in an attitude where you are *continually* trusting in God. Abraham traveled for three days not knowing where the Lord would tell him to stop and slay his son. Meaning that for three days, Abraham had the opportunity to be tempted to give up, go home, and save his son from death. But as the Lord revealed the location, the words out of Abraham's mouth give reason to why he is mentioned in Hebrews 11 (hall of faith). Abraham said, "*We* will go . . . and worship and *we* will come back." Abraham treated this test as an act of "worship" and, with bold faith, determined that though God had called him to kill his son, they would both return alive. We see in Hebrews 11 that Abraham reasoned that even if he were to kill his son, God would be mighty enough to raise him from the dead. That's trust and that's faith!

*So Abraham took the wood of the burnt offering and laid it on Isaac his son; and he took the fire in his hand, and a knife, and the two of them went together. But Isaac spoke to Abraham his father and said, "My father!" And he said, "Here I am, my son." Then he said, "Look, the fire and the wood, but where is the lamb for a burnt offering?" And Abraham said, "My son, God will provide for Himself the lamb for a burnt offering."*

I love the foreshadowing of the cross in this chapter. The "father" placed "wood" on the back of his "son." You see, God's love and compassion on humanity are revealed on every page of the Bible. But in this section of the scripture, I see another important principle: knowing that God will provide. It is one thing to trust that God can; it is entirely another thing to keep trusting and pressing in when you are not seeing the manifestation. So many believers have faith that God can meet their needs and provide for their lack, yet when the prayer is not answered right away or not manifested, discouragement settles in quickly and hope is lost. Ultimately we give up.

We have to develop the discipline that says, "I am gonna press in until I press through!" Even in the little things we must learn how to endure and press in until we see the promise of the Lord break through. The more victories you get under your belt, the easier it will be to endure and trust in the Lord. King David killed a lion and a bear before he killed a giant (1 Samuel 17:34), and we see that Abraham was faithful and trusted in God many times before this test came his way. Learn to trust God even in the little things and celebrate every victory whether big or small.

*So the two of them went together. Then they came to the place of which God had told him. And Abraham built an altar there and placed the wood in order; and he bound Isaac his son and laid him on the altar, upon the wood. And Abraham stretched out his hand and took the knife to slay his son.*
*But the Angel of the LORD called to him from heaven and said, "Abraham, Abraham!"*
*So he said, "Here I am." And He said, "Do not lay your hand on the lad, or do anything to him; for now I know that you fear God, since you have not withheld your son, your only son, from Me." Then Abraham lifted his eyes and looked, and there behind him was a ram caught in a thicket by its horns. So Abraham went and took the ram, and offered it up for a burnt offering instead of his son. And Abraham called the name of the place, The-LORD-Will-Provide; as it is said to this day, "In the Mount of the LORD it shall be provided."*

We know Abraham, Isaac, and Jacob as the patriarchs. Isaac, in this story, saw firsthand through his father what it means to trust in the Lord. Abraham passed on a spiritual living legacy to his son, and the motion was carried forward to his son.

I am a first-generation pastor, and my son, at the young age of five, loves to get onstage after his daddy does and proclaim that one day he is gonna be a preacher too. Our actions are being watched, by our families, coworkers, and strangers. We are walking testimonies and witnesses to the goodness and power of God. If we hold back, we miss out on the fulfillment of living our destinies and tell the world that God is one that holds back as well. We have a responsibility of overcoming the problems of the world with the truth of the Gospel so that the world may see that there is a God in heaven who wants His love and power released on His people.

## *Just Do It*

You and I have a loving and good Heavenly Father who desires to see His children live out the joys and power of heaven on this earth and in this life. We have been cleansed, filled, and set free by the blood of Jesus Christ. We have all the resources of heaven and every spiritual blessing at our disposal. We have the mind of Christ, the indwelling Holy Spirit, and the DNA of greatness beating in our hearts. The enemy has completely been defeated, and there is no wall, circumstance, or problem that can stop the coming move of God. We have been chosen for such a time as this.

My conclusion then is simply this: if God is really as big as we say He is and if we really are who He says we are, then the only thing stopping us . . . is us.

Let us chose this day to live with heaven-colored sunglasses, in which we learn to view life the way it should look like, a place marked with the love and power of God and a people whose hearts are for Him. The scripture in John 8:32 says, "The Truth shall make *you* free." It doesn't say "freedom will come to you." By living this life with the perspective of heaven, we can release what Jesus has already given us through His sacrifice and the truth of what God has said about us since the foundations of the earth.

On August 5, 2009, I received a phone call that a friend and fellow pastor had passed away. He had gone away to serve at a youth summer camp and passed while swimming with his youth group in a lake during a summer camp. Rory Graham, at age twenty-three, died far too early. The shock I felt was not necessarily that he was gone so soon, but that it was *he* that was gone too soon. There was no one else on the planet that I knew who was a stronger Christian than Rory. I had him preach many times in my youth group during the days I was a youth pastor, and everyone remembers him as the guy that preached without notes and spoke in scripture. Every time I bumped into him at a local Starbucks or restaurant, he had a different person that he was pouring into, praying for, and studying the scripture with. He was a phenomenal student, athlete, and pastor, and I simply could not understand why someone with the potential as Rory would be gone so soon.

I expected his funeral to be well attended. I didn't, however, anticipate to see what I saw. The large sanctuary of the church it was held at was full; there were several overflow rooms and even specialized tents for seating and video venues outside. Dozens of pastors, teachers, and community members gave speeches and participated in the service. I was so thankful to God when a pastor who was first up on the microphone said, "Some people can live a full life in only twenty-three years." There was an eruption of applause.

The greatest testimony for Rory was not the thousands he led to the Lord, the places he went, the sermons he preached or the impact he made; the greatest testimony was that he wasted no time and gave *everything* he had unto the Lord. He knew his identity in Christ. Rory understood the bigness of his God and, without hesitation or reservation, lived out his calling and destiny. You and I have the same promise.

*Copyedited by Kimberly Joyce Veloso*